FROM SLAVE TO PRIEST

Father Augustine Tolton

SISTER CAROLINE HEMESATH

FROM SLAVE
TO PRIEST

The Inspirational Story of
Father Augustine Tolton
(1854–1897)

With a Foreword by
Deacon Harold Burke-Sivers

IGNATIUS PRESS   SAN FRANCISCO

Originally published by
Franciscan Herald Press, Chicago
1973 by Franciscan Herald Press
Reprinted with permission

Published with ecclesiastical approval

Photographs for cover and pages, 2, 28, 38, 46, 89,
157, 198, and 222 were provided courtesy of the Tolton Collection at the Brenner Library of Quincy University, Quincy, Illinois.
Photographs on pages 54, 64, 90, 131, 132, 137,
152, 156, 163, 168, and 202 were reproduced from the
1973 edition.

Cover design by Riz Boncan Marsella

This book is dedicated to
the Most Reverend Joseph M. Mueller, D.D.
retired bishop of Sioux City
the friend of black people

CONTENTS

FOREWORD TO THE 2006 EDITION

Sister Caroline Hemesath's powerful narrative of Father Augustine Tolton's life is a poignant reminder that with God all things are possible. This welcome new edition reacquaints us with the first black American priest of the United States and chronicles the profound struggle for equality and acceptance faced by black Catholics in the postbellum era. Confronted with a succession of seemingly indomitable challenges (a narrow escape from slavery, his father's death, abject poverty, exclusion from American seminaries), Father Tolton's fervent desire to study Catholicism, his intense longing for the priesthood and his mother's loving support were the wellsprings from which he drew the strength to persevere.

Father Tolton knew that unconditional trust in God meant that he must become completely vulnerable before the God who made him. Father Tolton reveled in the folly of divine abandonment, confidently exposing the deepest parts of his soul before God who gave him the strength to exercise his priestly ministry under the weighty yoke of racism. He was a beacon of hope to black Catholics in the nineteenth century who were trying to find a home in the American Church. Father Tolton, in his abiding faith and selfless charity, was the instrument through which God's love shone brightly. The resplendent chorus, "I have come . . . not to do my own will, but the will of him who sent me" (Jn 6:38) echoed majestically throughout Father Tolton's brief life.

Despite the oppressive hardships placed upon Father Tolton by a culture firmly rooted in the arid soil of hatred and malevolence, God brought him out of the heart of darkness and used him as an instrument of grace. Father Tolton was a tireless messenger of the Gospel and "was not afraid to go into the deep South, where racial hatreds had reached a high pitch and where segregation was decreed by harsh laws." Despite the novelty of being the only black priest in an all-white clergy, the gifted Father Tolton was able effectively to convey the richness, beauty and truth of the Catholic faith, which penetrated even the hardest hearts ("Wherever he went, he was respected and honored").

When we look beneath the surface of our national life, we see that the septic undercurrent of racism flows largely unabated. Racism is alive and well, and is intricately woven into the fabric of American culture. But unlike the 1950s and '60s, where racism was overt, extreme, and statutorily institutionalized, the structure of racism today is more subtle and covert, exhibiting itself through outward manifestations of a now unconscious and tacit philosophy of dehumanization.

Since the 1960s and '70s, many black Catholics, in response to racism in the Church, have turned to and been heavily influenced by liberation theology, a Christian belief in the transcendent as a vehicle for social liberation. Liberation theology does not ask what the Church is, but rather what it means to be the Church in the context of liberating the poor and oppressed. As such, the Church's primary mission is to challenge oppression and identify herself with the poor. For liberation theology, the Magisterium (that is, the teaching authority of the Church) is part of the oppressive class by definition since, in this view, it does not participate in the class struggle. Ultimately, in this "liberation" version of Catholicism, faith is subordinate to political ideology, and the Church becomes an instrumental good rather than remaining an intrinsic good and the necessary means of salvation.

Father Tolton, a former slave become Catholic priest, knew well that the basis for any authentic theology of liberation must include the truth about Jesus, the Church and man's dignity. He endured years of frustration, humiliation, and rejection in a country boasting openness to religious freedom and tolerance. Despite the fact that slaves were "free", they were far from liberated. In Father Tolton's own words: "We are only a class—a class of dehumanized, brutalized, depersonalized beings." The nation failed the "freedom" litmus test rooted in its own Declaration of Independence, while the Catholic Church in America failed to live up to the tenets of her own creed and gospel by not recognizing that genuine liberation means freedom from the bondage of iniquity and sin.

With the assistance and support of several very persistent and undaunted priests, Father Tolton was finally accepted by the Catholic Church—in Rome! He thrived in the Eternal City where his priestly vocation was nurtured and where his gifts and talents were recognized, prompting even the prefect of the Sacred Congregation *de Propaganda Fide* to note what the American Church failed to appreciate: "Father Tolton is a good priest, reliable, worthy, and capable. You will discover that he is deeply spiritual and dedicated." For his part, Father Tolton acknowledged the great gift of his Catholic faith and, despite bitter trials and turmoil, remained faithful to the teachings of the Church. He was a visionary who saw far beyond race and politics, looking inward—into the heart of the Church herself. He taught, "The Catholic Church deplores a double slavery— that of the mind and that of the body. She endeavors to free us of both. . . . She is the Church for our people."

The life of Father Tolton is a study in faithful obedience. When the Vatican assigned Father Tolton to serve as a missionary priest in the United States, where he was "a slave, an outcast, a hated black", he obeyed in faith. His was not the faith of blind obedience, like that of an automaton or domesticated animal, but a spirit of faith that, as a child of our Heavenly Father—in complete humility and generosity —he continually strove to discern and fulfill the will of God under the loving guidance and direction of the Holy Spirit. It is precisely *duc et altum*—into the void, the unknown— that Father Tolton received his mission to be a fisher of men.

The greatest legacy of Father Augustine Tolton does not lie in the fact that he was a pioneer, the first black American priest in the United States. Yes, he was that—but he was so much more! Father Tolton loved and served the Lord with great fervor and intensity. He knew that God's love is so immense, its power so limitless, its embrace so tender and intimate, that Love Himself brings forth life. Father Tolton was a living testimony to God's creative, life-giving work.

Father Tolton serves as a role model for those who seek to be configured more perfectly to Christ. Amid great persecution, Father Tolton showed us that being configured to Christ means emptying ourselves so that God can fill us; it means exposing the weakest parts of who we are so that God can make us strong; it means becoming blind to the ways of this world so that Christ can lead us; it means dying to ourselves so that we can rise with Christ.

I pray that everyone who reads this biography will be inspired by Father Augustine Tolton, who, guided by the Holy Spirit, became a living example of what it means to be fully alive in our Catholic faith.

—Deacon Harold Burke-Sivers
Portland, Oregon
Holy Thursday, 2006

FOREWORD TO THE 1973 EDITION

The subject of this biography by Sister Caroline Hemesath, O.S.F., Father Augustine Tolton, is a much needed inspiration today—seventy-five years after the death of Father Tolton—for all Christians, especially for black Catholic youth and, in particular, for young blacks who would answer the call to the priesthood and religious life.

Born to a black Catholic slave family, whose church baptismal registry listing reads simply "colored child born on April 1 and the property of Steven Eliot", Father Tolton conquered almost insurmountable odds to become the first black Catholic priest in America, and at his death at forty-three, this pioneer black American priest left behind a legacy of holy service to his God, his Church, and his people.

Sister Caroline, through scholarly research and creativity borne of inspiration, has recorded that legacy, and it will inspire today's black Catholics who feel that, in the enlightened era of today's Church, walls of prejudice crumble too slowly. They will find hope in Christian dignity and fulfillment in service to God.

In American history, some written, but most unrecorded, thousands of blacks have achieved, against great odds, acceptance and success, making distinct contributions to our society and their fellowmen. Father Tolton's case was a different one. He found his opposition in the Church and among church people, where compassion should have offset established prejudice and ignorance. It was his lot to disprove the myth that young black men could not assume the responsibility of the Catholic priesthood.

PREFACE

My interest in Augustine Tolton dates from the year 1933, the first of my nine years as a teacher of black children in Chicago. While making a study of black Catholicism I learned about Saint Monica's Church, which no longer existed, and its first pastor, a black, who had died thirty-six years earlier.

In the course of that study it was my privilege to speak with persons who were Father Tolton's parishioners—people who had been closely associated with the priest, with his mother and sister. I interviewed Mother Katherine Drexel, who helped Father Tolton financially, and also spoke to Sisters who had conducted Saint Monica's School. I conferred with Father Joseph Eckert, S.V.D., who became known as the "second Father Tolton", and also corresponded with him later.

I corresponded with Mrs. Caecilia Hubbard Barnett, a contemporary of Father Tolton and a member of Saint Monica's parish. Her vivid memories, dating from her childhood, provided invaluable information.

Materials were made available to me by the Josephite Fathers, Baltimore, Maryland; by Father Landry Genosky, O.F.M., archivist of Quincy College, Quincy, Illinois; by the Sisters of Saint Francis, Saint Mary's Hospital, Hoboken, New Jersey; by the Sisters of Mercy, Mercy Hospital, Chicago, Illinois; and by the School Sisters of Notre Dame, whose motherhouse is at Mequon, Wisconsin. Among these archival documents were seven letters written by Father Tolton.

Upon the recommendation of the Most Reverend Joseph M. Mueller, bishop of Sioux City, Cardinal Gregory Agagianian, Prefect of the Sacred Congregation *de Propaganda Fide*, permitted me to use documents from the archives of the Sacred Congregation.

Those passages in the biography that are imaginative recreations rest solidly on the foundation of research. The atmosphere and tone reproduced in these developed naturally from living long and intensively—through letters, documents, and recollections—in the world of Augustine Tolton.

During his lifetime and at the time of his death, Father Tolton was known as "the first colored priest of the United States" inasmuch as both his father and his mother were black. Since many now use the term "colored" or "black" also of mulattoes, and there were mulatto priests in the United States before Father Tolton, we have called the latter "the first black priest of the United States". Three "black" sons of an Irishman in Georgia—Michael Morris Healy and a mulatto slave mother—were ordained priests in the 1850s. They were James Augustine, Patrick, and Sherwood. The first was ordained a priest in 1854, the year in which Father Tolton was born, and in 1875 was named bishop of Portland, Maine (see Anne Tansey, "The Black Bishop of Maine", *The Catholic Digest*, July 1972, pp. 103–6).

It is impossible to give adequate thanks and recognition to all who have so generously helped me with the research necessary for this book. But I am sincerely grateful for all the encouragement and assistance that enable me to tell the story of a truly important American.

Sister Caroline Hemesath, O.S.F.

I

THE WEDDING CELEBRATION

The John Manning plantation in Mead County, Kentucky, was jumping with excitement. During that whole week in the summer of 1849, carriage after carriage had pulled up depositing relatives and friends of the "first" Catholic families for the wedding of Susan Manning and Stephen Eliot. The Reverend Charles Coomes officiated at the marriage, which took place in the nearby parish church at Flint Island. And now after the ceremony, the handsome mansion and broad lawns, gaily lighted and festooned, welcomed the guests. They met in the stately parlors of the house or gathered in groups under the magnolia trees. House servants in colorful livery and slaves glided in and out of the "big house", ensuring the comfort and well-being of every visitor. There were music and laughter, lively conversation and friendly banter. The long tables were heaped with choice foods and rare wines. While bride and bridegroom moved among the guests, everyone participated in the festivities— games and contests, dancing, singing, feasting—lasting far into the night.

Susan was the youngest daughter of the John Mannings. Her father had died when she was a child. Later her mother married Stephen Burch and promptly transferred the prop-

overseer and then strode back to the mansion to rejoin the wedding guests. The marked slaves were cast into a state of utter dejection, panic, and terror. The paint signs foreboded one of several possibilities: punishment, additional hours of labor, or auctioning (that is, being "sold down the river").

The wedding celebration was at its height when the bride, leaning on the arm of her tall bridegroom, entered the drawing room to admire and accept the wedding presents. Piled high on tables and sideboards was an array of wearing apparel, household utensils, foodstuffs, ornaments, linens, and furniture. The delighted young couple tried to express thanks, but their words were lost in the hubbub of voices. They made an attempt to single out the donors of each gift, but the cheering guests impeded their attempts. A shower of applause followed the unwrapping of each item among the gifts. Little squeals of happiness came from the overjoyed bride, and beaming smiles from the bridegroom.

Then came the moment for Stephen Eliot to present his gift to his bride. Proudly he unfolded the document which authorized ownership of lands and holdings: a farm and buildings in Missouri where they would live. "It is located near the small town of Brush Creek in Ralls County", he said, "and about five miles from Hannibal."

Susan was radiant with joy; in the exuberance of her delight she clutched her husband's arm and whispered in his ear, "I have a gift for you too."

This was the part of her wedding celebration for which the bride had waited with greatest eagerness. Grasping Stephen's arm more firmly, she hurried him away from the crowd. A short distance from the mansion stood the so-called meeting hall. The huge double doors of the barnlike buildings were locked. Susan led her husband toward this entrance and ordered an overseer to open the doors. "Look, Stephen," she cried exultantly, "ours—my marriage dowry. We can take them with us. They belong to us." Huddled in a corner of the hall and brought there for exhibition was a batch of slaves, the forearm of each showing a blotch of red paint. One of those slaves was Martha Jane Chisley.

The wedding celebration was over. Most of the guests had departed, and preparations were being made for the journey of the wedded couple to their Missouri home. The baggage, which included everything they needed to set up housekeeping, was loaded on horse-drawn vehicles. A cart attached to the last wagon served to transport the shackled slaves. The overland journey westward through three Kentucky counties required several days. At the Mississippi River bank, wagons with baggage and slaves would be transferred to riverboats and rafts.

When the travelers were ready to proceed, the slaves were loaded onto the cart. Martha Jane wept convulsively at the thought of being separated from her parents and brother. No one paid the slightest attention to her sorrow. At the moment of departing, her brother Charley, frenzied with grief, came running from the slave quarters. He jumped onto the cart and caught Martha Jane in a viselike embrace; he shrieked in desperation.

The overseer ordered the youth to leave, and when his words were neither heard nor heeded, the angered man brought his whip down on the young slave's back. Charley's grasp loosened, and he fell from the cart in a crumpled heap at the feet of the overseer. Martha Jane, catching a glimpse of the whip raised a second time, turned aside swiftly to avoid the painful sight. Her face was distorted in agony and utter despair, and her heartbreaking moans were lost amid the shouts of farewells and the tumult of leave-taking.

As the cart jolted along and the days wore on, Martha Jane's courage revived. Crossing the Mississippi River gave the slave girl her first experience of nature's grandeur. She raised her dark face heavenward. It was a study in Christian faith.

2

IN QUEST OF FREEDOM

The Stephen Eliot lands in Ralls County, Missouri, adjoined those of another Catholic family named Hager. One of the Hager slaves, Peter Paul Tolton, had been purchased at a Hannibal, Missouri, auction. He had been baptized by the Reverend Peter Paul Lefebre, a missionary priest whose headquarters from 1834 to 1837 were at Saint Paul, Missouri, and was extremely proud of the fact that he had received the priest's Christian name.

From the time he was a little boy Peter Paul had been a field worker in the Hager grainfields or a handyman employed in the master's distillery. Like his fellow slaves, old and young, male and female, Peter's life had been made up of the day after day and year after year monotony and drudgery of bondage. His world consisted solely of vast fields, ugly distillery buildings, and a row of slave cabins. Every summer Peter Paul saw the fields of yellow grain dotted with half-naked Negroes working briskly under a burning sun. He knew that the rye grown on the Hager lands was used solely for the manufacture of whiskey. Year-round slave labor was needed for seeding, cultivating, harvesting, and distilling. Peter Paul had endured endless hours cutting the ripe grain with sickle or scythe, binding it into bundles and loading it on wagons drawn by slaves. He had helped on the threshing floor, where, by means of laborious flaying, the grain was separated from the chaff.

The only respite in Peter Paul Tolton's shackled existence and his sole schooling was the rudimentary religious instruction provided by his master. However, the more Peter shaped his life in accordance with the Decalogue, the more perplexed and rankled he became at the sight of the flagrant transgressions of these same God-ordained laws by white people—free people—Christian people.

Besides being a strong and faithful worker, Peter Paul Tolton, the illiterate slave, had keen intelligence and an active mind. In those pre-Civil War days, when political and social unrest, strife and violence were mounting in all areas of government, when ideas were pitted against ideals, when opinions clashed with facts, and might was substituted for right, hate-ridden views dealing with the explosive issues of the day seeped into the slave quarters.

Often during the long hours of silent work in the fields, Peter Paul thought and reasoned; around the distillery where traders and propagandists talked and argued, Peter Paul listened. By and by he became fairly well acquainted with then current views of antislavery, secession, insurrection, and war. He sympathized with the life-risking abolitionists, and he believed the scaffold words of John Brown: "I am now quite *certain* that the crimes of this guilty land will never be purged *away* but by blood." Piecing together the grapevine whisperings of newly acquired slaves and the information he had gained elsewhere, Peter Paul came to a conclusion that coincided with the thoughts harbored by some of the most famous men of that age, namely, all men are equal—*including* Negroes.

From time to time Peter Paul Tolton had toyed with the idea of escaping from his master and reaching free territory. Other slaves had made a safe getaway from brutal masters. Why couldn't he? Moreover, Peter Paul was by now imbued with the idea that people must be converted into acknowledging that all men, *including blacks*, are equal and that they have equal rights and privileges. He knew about the Underground Railroad (the means provided by sympathetic whites to assist fugitive slaves), though not by that designation. He had seen just too many lash-scarred slaves, nor had he himself been spared the master's whip.

Peter Paul was determined to get away; he resolved to risk punishment—even death—just to break away from the intolerable situation of slavery. Long hours in the field or at the distillery gave him time to formulate in more detail his plan of escape. But one day his ruminations were interrupted by a cry for help coming from a nearby field. As he hurried across the field, Peter Paul saw an emaciated slave boy who had collapsed, apparently from sheer exhaustion. He lay lifeless in the arms of a fellow worker—Martha Jane Chisley.

Beneath the dust, perspiration, and utter weariness on the upturned face of the girl, Peter glimpsed something rare and inestimably precious—Christian compassion. It was the most beautiful sight he had ever seen.

During the weeks that followed, Peter's lot seemed less burdensome to him; the work in the grainfields was not so toilsome, and the hours of labor seemed shorter. All thoughts and schemes for an escape from his owner vanished. His whole outlook changed; life took on a new meaning. Peter Paul had fallen in love.

In the spring of 1851 Peter Paul Tolton and Martha Jane Chisley were married in Saint Peter's Church, Brush Creek, Missouri, by Father John O'Sullivan. The respective owners of the couple consented to the marriage under this agreement: the Toltons would live in a cabin on the Eliot farm, and Peter would remain a slave of the Hager family. All children born of the union would be the property of Stephen Eliot.

After the marriage Peter Paul and Martha Jane had to work

Martha Jane hustled the frightened children into a dilapidated rowboat, paddled to the opposite shore, and landed in the free state of Illinois.

In later years Augustine Tolton often recalled the passage across the wide river. His mother, wholly inexperienced at rowing, struggled frantically with the oars and caused the small craft to veer crazily from side to side. They had scarcely succeeded in pushing away from the Missouri shore when they heard the angry voices of Confederate men shouting threats and curses. One of the pursuers raised his musket and fired repeatedly at the little boat. Undaunted by the whistling bullets, the mother ordered the children to lie flat in the bottom of the vessel. The baby screamed from sheer bewilderment and fright. The boys did what they could to calm her, although they also cried all the way. Relying entirely on the protection of divine power, the determined mother clung to the oars and succeeded in placing a safe distance between the boat and the chagrined slave hunters.

Even though Martha Jane had been without food for days, she had the strength to bring her children to safety. One by one she helped them from the swaying rowboat, and together they stepped from slavery forever. Kneeling upon the ground, the valiant woman gathered the weeping children into her arms. Tears streamed down her dark cheeks as she said, "Now you are free. Never, never forget the goodness of the Lord."

3

THE PRICE OF FREEDOM

As a contingent of black and white workmen on the "grave-yard shift" were hurrying toward an Illinois wharf, their customary talking and guffawing were interrupted by the loud wailing of children. Peering into the direction from which the sounds seemed to come, the men discovered a black woman with three small children in a huddle beside the road. The presence of this group at this unusual time, in the deserted area, together with their shabby mud-splashed clothes and signs of distress, labeled them unmistakably as runaway slaves.

The workmen formed a half circle before the forlorn family and began to comfort the whimpering children by offering them food from their lunch sacks. At first Martha Jane was thoroughly frightened when the men approached, but their concern and obvious sympathy gave her the courage to tell them who she was, where she had come from, and where she wanted to go.

"Keep going north, Mrs. Tolton," said one of the group, pointing in that direction, "and just follow the river."

"Quincy's a good twenty miles from here", said another. "This here road leads right into the place."

For the first time in her life, Martha Jane heard herself called Mrs. Tolton, and despite her weariness that gave her new courage and a sense of dignity. One of the laborers as

the news of victory came new hope for her, but as time dragged on, resignation began to take the place of waiting; memory, the place of reunion.

Mrs. Tolton knew that thousands of other slaves, just as her husband, had risked the dangers of escape to enlist in the northern army. She understood that they were determined to save the Union and abolish slavery and that they wanted to raise the status of the blacks. Official lists of casualties showed that among the thousands of soldiers sacrificed in the Civil War, 63,178 were blacks. One of these was Peter Paul Tolton.

Again and again the Tolton children wanted to hear their mother recite the story of their father, his courage and bravery. "He was so good and kind", she would begin. "He said he would make the world a better place to live in. And when he stood beside the bed where you three were sleeping", she went on in a half whisper now and blinking away the tears, "he said, 'I will fight for them, make us all free, and then come back home.'"

The wide-eyed children always waited breathlessly for that homecoming, and in his later life, Augustine referred to this as his father's last testament: "They must not be slaves; they must learn to read and write; they must have a better life than we had."

Peter Paul Tolton lay buried, unknown and unsung, in some lonely grave, but the memory of him—his purpose in life and the price he paid to reach his goal—lay enshrined in the heart of his son, a courageous ideal to live up to.

But just now Mrs. Tolton's biggest worry was to get a job to support herself and her children. "You can easily get a job at Harris", her friends assured her. "Grownups get anywheres from five dollars to nine dollars a week, and children get fifty cents a week if they do good work", they volunteered.

Harris was a sprawling tobacco factory located at the junction of Quincy's Fifth and Ohio Streets. At the sound of the morning whistle, more than three hundred employees, blacks and whites, began work in the various shops, offices, and shipping departments of the company. When Mrs. Tolton appeared at the employment office window, she was immediately hired. Later Charley and Augustine, at the ages of ten and nine, respectively, began work at the same factory.

During the first year mother and sons worked together as stemmers. They stood for ten hours a day for a six-day week as tobacco stalks three to four feet in length were piled on their table. Augustine remarked later that the heap never became smaller because other factory hands continually replenished the supply. He recalled that the stems, large and small, had to be removed so that the green leaves were ready for the roller. A black man named Mr. Pleasant supervised the Toltons at the stemming table. Augustine declared that the name fitted the man exactly.

All the factory workers soon learned that the whole process of tobacco manufacturing was carried on during the eight or nine so-called seasonal months. Curing, stemming, rolling, fermenting, and drying, all constantly in progress, always kept the place filled with nicotine fumes with a nauseating odor. Workers breathed the clinging stench of the curing and fermenting areas; they detested the smells, which pervaded every room and shop, as well as the outside factory area for blocks around. After the sound of the whistle that signaled the end of the work day, weary laborers in sweaty and reeking clothes poured out of every entrance, carrying tobacco odors wherever they went.

Back in the ghetto, Mrs. Tolton planned the education of her children. Although illiterate, she knew the Ten Commandments and she taught her family how to observe them. Prayers she had learned as a slave were said regularly every day with the added incentive: "We must never forget to thank the Lord for his goodness, and we must ask him to

Saint Boniface Church, Quincy

take care of us always." Mrs. Tolton also taught her children how to sing. Hymns and plantation songs dating from her own childhood were a part of everyday living in the Tolton household. "I learned my praying and my singing at my mother's knee", was Augustine's lifelong boast.

From the beginning of their stay in Quincy, Mrs. Tolton and her children joined other black Catholics who attended Saint Boniface Church. They usually congregated in one corner, but from the outset they felt sure that Father Herman Schaeffermeyer, pastor of the 2,000-member German parish, was not opposed to their presence. For the benefit of his people, most of whom were immigrants, Father Schaeffermeyer read the Epistles and Gospels in German and also gave the sermon in that language. Then, for the sake of non-German worshipers, he read the Gospel and summarized the sermon in English.

Because Augustine Tolton was a regular attendant, he gradually learned German. He loved to hear the Gospel stories and to retell them at home. When dramatizing the parables, such as the Prodigal Son or the Good Samaritan, for the children of the neighboring alleys, Augustine used both German and English words. In the "staging" of these and other Gospel narratives, he always played all the roles himself. His playmates were expected to do no more than listen and respond with a loud *Amen* whenever he gave the cue.

During the winter of 1863, while the tobacco shops were closed, suffering and grief came to the Toltons. Charley, always weak and sickly, caught cold and developed pneumonia. Medicines prescribed by the doctor did not help. Day and night Mrs. Tolton sat beside the bed of her sick son. Neighbors and friends came to help, but they could do nothing. Ten-year-old Charley died.

The mother was heartbroken. But for the sake of Augustine and Anne, she hid her sorrow and went back to work. In accordance with her true and simple faith, Mrs. Tolton decided that her children should attend a Catholic school; she felt that this would involve no more of a problem than did their attendance at Saint Boniface Church. At the parish school Sisters of Notre Dame taught the girls and smaller boys; the older boys were instructed by priests and laymen.

In 1865, when Augustine was eleven years old, Mrs. Tolton accompanied him to school and asked to have him enrolled for the three winter months. On this occasion she met Sister Chrysologus, who was to be Augustine's teacher; Sister Seraphine, the superior; and Father Schaeffermeyer. "Shure, shure, ve vill take him in", said the pastor in his heavy accent. Mrs. Tolton smiled gratefully and looked at her son with evident maternal pride. Augustine sat on the edge of the chair and twisted his cap. He looked shyly from one person to another without lifting his head. This was his first experience in a school. The only other teaching he had received was the Sunday morning catechism class conducted by Sivella Eliot, who taught prayers and the rudiments of religion to her parents' slaves. Trembling with fear and excitement, Augustine followed Sister Chrysologus to the classroom.

By admitting Augustine Tolton, Father Schaeffermeyer became the first priest of Quincy to allow a black child into an all-white school. He was, of course, wholly unprepared for the reaction of his German congregation. Parents threatened to withdraw their children from the school, to discontinue their support of the parish and even their membership in it. The unchristian sentiments of the parents influenced the children and made them feel free to mistreat

Augustine. They began to taunt him because he could neither read nor write; they mimicked his accent. The girls tit-
tered and whispered, holding their noses in derision while
pointing fingers at him. "You stink, you stink", they yelled
at him on the playground as they dashed toward him; then,
fearing that Augustine might retaliate, they fled in another
direction and shouted insults from a distance.

"Look at the dirty nigger", hissed the boys in the classroom as they pelted him with paper wads when Sister was
not looking. Unable to defend himself, Augustine slumped
down in utter dejection, and several times he broke out in
uncontrollable sobs. Sister Chrysologus comforted him as
best she could and kept him in the classroom when school
was dismissed just to protect him from his tormentors. During these times she gave him special lessons in reading and
writing. At this time, too, she discovered Augustine's ability in speaking both German and English, and soon he was
learning to read and write both languages. It was primarily
through this after-school instruction that the boy acquired
his love for learning.

Augustine's mother was also fully aware of the antagonism that his presence in the school had aroused. Actually it
was a part of the hostility shown toward all the blacks who
attended Saint Boniface Church. Father Schaeffermeyer and
the Sisters received anonymous threatening letters. Someone
hurled a rock at the parish rectory and shattered a window.
Soon the news spread that a petition to the bishop of the
diocese was being planned demanding that Father Schaeffermeyer be removed from the parish.

Mrs. Tolton was bewildered and heartbroken. "Augustine," she said to her son, who had attended Saint Boniface
School less than one month, "I think we better tell Father

and the Sisters that you will not go back to the Catholic
School."

Mother and son called on the kind priest and the Sisters
and thanked them for their efforts. "Father," asked Mrs. Tolton respectfully, "would it perhaps be better if for a while
we did not go to Saint Boniface Church? We could maybe
go to another Catholic church at least for a while."

Father Schaeffermeyer hung his head in shame and sorrow. "Ja, ja," he said in a trembling whisper, "maybe it vould
be better." For a long time after the disappointed mother and
her son left the rectory, Father Schaeffermeyer sat in gloomy
silence. "I do not understand my people", he sighed, bow-
ing his head.

4

THE SPIRIT BREATHES WHERE IT WILL

From the year of its establishment in 1839, Saint Boniface Church of Quincy suffered a period of storm and stress that lasted more than twenty years. With the appointment of Father Schaeffermeyer as pastor in 1858, the parish entered upon an era of peace and progress, as was evidenced by its phenomenal growth both in membership and physical plant.

Prior to his immigration from Germany to America, Father Schaeffermeyer had labored fifteen years as a priest in his native country. A tireless devotion to duty manifested itself in the many signal improvements and reforms he inaugurated in the cause of religion and education. As pastor of the first and largest Catholic church in Quincy, Father Schaeffermeyer felt responsible for all the people in the community. He showed his concern for everyone by using both German and English to instruct the congregation. He made no distinctions by race, color, or nationality. His solicitude for all people was proof of his singlehearted zeal.

Father Schaeffermeyer was keenly disappointed and hurt by the violent opposition of his parishioners when, two years after the Emancipation Proclamation, he admitted Augustine Tolton to Saint Boniface's parochial school. Neither the priest's European background nor his study of American political philosophy had prepared him for the storm of protest, prejudice, and race hatred that had resulted from the performance of what he saw as his simple pastoral obligation. In later years there were always overtones of regret and sorrow in Father Schaeffermeyer's voice as he recalled the incident: "I can see them yet—mother and son—Mrs. Tolton's arm flung around the boy's shoulders—walking down the sidewalk after we drove them out."

From the day Augustine Tolton withdrew from Saint Boniface's School, Father Schaeffermeyer took a special and very paternal interest in the boy. Often when he saw Augustine hurrying to and from the Harris tobacco factory, the priest stopped to say a few friendly words. At other times he would fall in step with the factory hand and walk several blocks of Quincy's streets just to express his concern.

In the course of these walks Father Schaeffermeyer learned a good deal about cigar making. Augustine worked in the curing and drying departments and received three dollars a week for labor far too hard for him. Day after day, as Augustine described it for the priest, the workers had to lift long, heavy tobacco stalks and hang them on poles to dry—that is, allow the surplus nicotine to escape. And of course, the barns in which this processing was done were constantly filled with obnoxious fumes: to prevent the tobacco leaves from cracking, moisture was added, and the resulting fermentation caused suffocating stenches. "We wear masks in the barns", Augustine told the priest. "Smells bad all the time—lots of people working in there get sick."

Mr. Harris, brother of the proprietor, supervised the work in the departments to which Augustine was assigned. On several occasions Father Schaeffermeyer spoke with Mr. Harris concerning Augustine's job. The priest hoped to secure better working conditions for the young worker. Mr. Harris was interested and promised to do all he could for Augustine, whom he described as "our most reliable factory hand".

During several seasons Augustine worked in the sorting or grading rooms. Tobacco leaves that had been stemmed, dried, and cured were classified according to size, color, and texture for cigars, cigarettes, pipe tobacco, chewing tobacco, and snuff. Augustine described the work in the grading rooms as "easier to do—but much bad talk".

During the winter months of 1868, when the factory was closed for the usual three months, Augustine enrolled in the all-black Lincoln School. This small log cabin was a state maintained institution, but the equipment was primitive; no standard qualifications were required for teachers, since compulsory education for blacks was unknown. Consequently attendance was irregular and erratic, especially on the part of older, working pupils. Classes in elementary reading, penmanship, and numbers were conducted by teachers whose scholarship in many cases was not above that of the older pupils.

Several factors combined to make Augustine's initiation at this school a bitter experience. Fourteen years old and tall for his age, he was still not ready for his normal grade; moreover, he was very dark-skinned, and he reeked of stale tobacco. Younger boys and girls who could read and write far better than he pointed this out with open ridicule, and this added to his humiliation and frustration. Mulattoes (numerous in this district) called him "black boy" and "the African" —a subtle sting and incisive thrust understood fully only by the victim. And, finally, with the aim of provoking a fight in which Augustine could prove his mettle, older boys made snide remarks about his parentage. "Where's yer father? Don't you have no father?" they taunted.

Augustine's attempts to tell about his father were interrupted by shouts of "his mother's a whore" and followed by a chorus of jeers. When Augustine tried to defend himself to avenge his mother, the sport turned to catcalls of "bastard" or "coward" and "blackie". But his initiation eventually ended in the acceptance of the newcomer to their games and classes. Augustine came to school each day of the first month and made progress in reading and writing, and, strange to say, mostly with the help of his previous tormentors.

Father Peter McGirr, pastor of Saint Peter's Church,
who promised an education to Augustine

Shortly after the unfortunate experience at Saint Boniface School, Mrs. Tolton and her family had affiliated with Saint Peter's Church, located on Eighth and Maine Streets. Father Peter McGirr, a young and zealous pastor, welcomed them warmly. There was relatively little opposition to the presence of blacks in Saint Peter's Church: first, because they occupied a segregated area in one corner of the building in accordance with their own preference; and secondly, the indomitable will of Father McGirr, who befriended the blacks, was not really opposed.

Peter McGirr, who was born in Ireland, came to America when he was fifteen years old. He studied for the priesthood and was ordained in 1861 by Bishop Damien Juncker for the diocese of Alton (Springfield). A year later he was appointed pastor of a twenty-year-old parish in Quincy, then known as Saint Patrick's, with a membership of fewer than two hundred Irish families scattered in and around the city. A man of few words and many deeds, Father McGirr began his thirty-five-year ministry with an unspoken motto: "I'm here to help you, and I know what you need."

With indefatigable zeal sustained by a magnificent Irish temper, Father McGirr inaugurated a series of improvements. As early as 1864 there were 250 children in attendance at Saint Peter's newly erected school. They were taught by Sisters of Notre Dame. A citywide census planned by the pastor revealed the need of a new church and a parish cemetery. By 1870, when membership in Saint Peter's parish had reached 1,500, an imposing edifice dedicated to Saint Peter (one biographer says to Father McGirr) replaced the earlier small clapboard structure. Father McGirr did his best to break down the clannish, nationalistic attitude of his compatriots and welcomed non-Irish families to the parish. His sole argument, "Christ died for all", reassured the "outsiders", especially black families. The same argument usually silenced any malcontented parishioners.

The black contingent in the church increased, and this pleased the pastor but probably displeased many of his people. Mrs. Tolton with Augustine and Anne managed to be the first to arrive at the church for Sunday services and the last to leave. By this practice she hoped to avert the offensive thrusts of "Get out, niggers" covertly directed at them by some less-than-Christian worshipers. But she was not able to shield her children entirely from this ignominious treatment. Augustine was subjected to many abusive remarks when, inadvertently, he wandered into select white circles. His reactions to offensive and stinging talk were a courteous apology and a hurried exit. From the time he was a small boy he learned, from an association with the white race, to accept the fact that degradation and contempt were the common lot of God's black children.

Sixteen-year-old Mary Ann Davis, to whom Augustine always referred as his "sister", was a victim of lingering tuberculosis and had been bedridden for many months. When, during the winter of 1868, her mounting fever warranted the last rites of the Church, Father McGirr was summoned to her deathbed. He arrived at the shack to anoint the girl and to say the prayers for the dying. Then, as he comforted the bereaved members of the household it was that Father McGirr spoke to Augustine Tolton for the first time, although Father Schaeffermeyer had on several occasions extolled the boy's unusual qualities.

After Father McGirr had led prayers for the departed soul, Augustine accompanied him to the door and out into the street. In their conversation the priest learned that Augustine was a regular factory worker at the Harris Tobacco Company and that now, during the winter shutdown, was attending Lincoln public school. The priest's surprise turned into righteous indignation: "You go to a public school? Why, you are Catholic and must stop going there. Next week I want to see you in Saint Peter's School", he said in a kind but decidedly firm voice. "You will lose your faith in the non-Catholic place."

Augustine looked in puzzlement at Father McGirr. "But I went to that school—the Lincoln School—only about two months," he said in a small, timid voice, "and I am still Catholic."

Father McGirr soon realized that he had spoken on impulse. He remembered the difficulties encountered by Father Schaeffermeyer a few years earlier. It may be wise, he thought, to proceed with caution. The priest prepared himself for any unpleasantness or trouble that might arise, but he redoubled his resolution in advance not to be intimidated or dissuaded by his parishioners. This venture, he concluded, would be a perfect object lesson of his own frequent assertion that "Christ died for all men". Yes, he would practice what he preached. To begin with, he would call on the Sisters who taught at the school and enlist their cooperation.

The first religious teachers to staff the parochial schools of Quincy were the School Sisters of Notre Dame, whose motherhouse was then located in Milwaukee, Wisconsin. Mother Mary Caroline, first commissary general of this community in the United States, on the advice of Bishop Juncker, had established a convent on Quincy's Eighth and Vermont Streets in 1861. Sisters engaged as teachers in the several parishes lived in this convent, which was known as Saint Mary's Institute.

When Father McGirr called at the convent, he asked to see the three teachers of Saint Peter's School: Sister Herlinde Sick, Sister Sebastian Kock, and Sister Eustachia Downing. When they arrived he stated the purpose of his visit. "Sisters," he began firmly, "a Negro boy named Augustine Tolton will start school here next week. If any of the other children or their parents have anything to say, send them to me." Father McGirr explained the case further: "He has been going to the Lincoln Public School for two months. Because he works in the tobacco factory, he can go to school only in the winter. Most likely he will be behind in his studies."

Augustine Tolton was assigned to a classroom with pupils of his own age. Sister Herlinde, the teacher, was especially enthusiastic over the new "apostolate". Together with the other two Sisters she planned ways and means by which disturbances might be averted and, above all, how to make the black pupil feel at home and to protect him from harm. Before Augustine arrived, each Sister had instructed her pupils and encouraged them to treat the newcomer as they would like to be treated and to love and help him because this was pleasing to God. The Sisters also reminded the white children of the punishment they would incur if they displayed the slightest ill will. "We had no trouble at all in school", said Sister Herlinde. "It was the parents who raised the objections."

Father McGirr received the threatening anonymous letters he anticipated. He was told that children would be withdrawn from the school, parish support would be discontinued, and membership in the parish would be terminated. Some wrote that they would leave the Church and give up their religion entirely. Every letter of that tenor was immediately consigned to the wastebasket; every caller at the rectory was asked to state his business before he was admitted to the priest's study. Any cases dealing with opposition to the black pupil in the school were promptly dismissed. "His Reverence be too busy entirely", explained the housekeeper. "He will answer your questions in the Sunday sermon; he will now." A parish delegation composed of several men and women were left standing in the snow, despite the insistent sound of the rectory knocker.

Until the furor died down, Father McGirr's Sunday sermons were masterpieces of eloquence. He explained Catholic doctrine and added subtle barbed applications. "If you did it to the least of my brethren, you did it to me!" he thundered. "Let the children come to me", he pleaded, and on several occasions he dramatically tied millstones around the necks of sinners. Father McGirr literally enacted the story of the man who fell among robbers, and he artfully planned to have his sermons on charity end with a vociferous "Depart from me into everlasting fire!" The crafty speaker chose exemplifying details and supporting materials from sources far removed from "the Negro question", but it was precisely the Tolton case which provided inspiration and drew forth his eloquence. In the management of this affair Father McGirr defied civic regulations and municipal ordinances that had been set up to separate blacks from white groups. He was an integrationist of the first order.

At the time Augustine Tolton began to attend Saint Peter's School, Mrs. Tolton moved from the tiny shanty in the black district to a brick shed behind the local livery stable on 818 Main Street. This brought the family closer to Saint Peter's Church and School.

Sister Herlinde soon discovered that Augustine was far behind in his studies and that he was able to read and write only on an elementary level. With Christian compassion she concealed this fact from the other children and arranged to give the boy private instructions before and after school hours. All the rest of his life Augustine cherished the memory of the Sisters at Saint Peter's School, each one of whom had some part in the special lessons he received at odd hours. "As long as I was in that school," he said, "I was safe. Everyone was kind to me. I learned the alphabet, spelling, reading, arithmetic, and other things in Saint Peter's School, and partly by hearing others read around our home."

During the first month at Saint Peter's School, Augustine memorized the Latin prayers for Mass, and Sister Sebastian trained him to be an altar boy. When the three winter months of school were over, Augustine was due at the tobacco factory to continue his work in the barns until the next winter —a pattern he was to follow for the next five years. To his great joy, however, he was allowed to serve the priest at Mass—those Masses celebrated before his work hours— at Saint Peter's Church and sometimes, at the invitation of Father Schaeffermeyer, the early Mass at Saint Boniface as well. Occasionally he served Mass at Saint Mary's Institute.

Although Augustine did not know the meaning of all the Latin words and phrases he had learned from his book, he did know the meaning of the first words he used at every Mass. A new light glowed in his eyes and his heart beat with high and unspoken aspirations as he repeated the words to himself day after day: "I will go to the altar of God, I will go to the altar of God—to God who gives joy. . . ."

5

THE DIVINE INVITATION

Sixteen-year-old Augustine Tolton wandered in and out of Saint Peter's Church. It was the afternoon of the feast of Corpus Christi—the day on which he received his first Holy Communion. All the other boys and girls of his class had gone to their homes, but Augustine could not tear himself away. He wanted to remain close to the place of that morning's joy, near the altar still bedecked with lights and flowers. Kneeling in the empty and very quiet church whose sanctuary lamp proclaimed the Divine Presence, Augustine relived every part of the ceremony: once again he entered the church in procession; he heard the resounding organ music and noticed the crowds of worshipers; he sang the hymns again, pronounced the baptismal vows, attended the class, and received Holy Communion. He recalled the words from the Gospel, "He who eats my flesh and drinks my blood abides in me and I in him. He who eats this bread shall live forever" (Jn 6:57, 59). He could still hear Father McGirr's sermon, which began with "My dear First Communicants!" Quoting the scriptural account of the Last Supper, the priest gave a fuller explanation and meaning of the Sacrifice of the Mass and the Holy Eucharist. Augustine remembered that his heart leaped with a strange exhilaration when Father McGirr told the meaning of the words: "Do this in commemoration of me."

Old Saint Peter's Church, Quincy

Augustine was completely oblivious to the here and now; his thoughts soared and ended up in a whirlwind of hopes and plans. He envisioned himself as another Father Schaeffermeyer, as another Father McGirr; he imagined himself at the altar offering Mass and speaking before the congregation about the "goodness of the Lord". He reveled in this ecstasy for a while, and then his mind suddenly plunged back into the world of reality. He was a black—an outcast—a runaway slave—a tobacco factory hand—the breadwinner for a poverty-stricken family.

From his rectory window Father McGirr saw Augustine come out of the church. His hands thrust into his pockets, the boy walked briskly to and fro on the parish grounds; every now and then he stopped, looked wistfully at the structure, and let his eyes travel up and down the spire.

"What are you thinking about, Augustine?" It was the voice of Father McGirr, who had burst out of the rectory.

Augustine, startled for a moment, flashed a pleased smile. "Oh, Father, I think of many things today", he answered excitedly. "Like what I want to be—and what I would like to do. I don't know how to say it, but I want to be something very great."

Father McGirr, who had observed Augustine for some time—at school, at church, and on the street—was convinced that the lad was meant for the priesthood. Several months earlier, when preparing the pupils for First Communion, he first discovered the genuine faith and integrity of Augustine Tolton. At that time he told Sister Herlinde that the youth was "the best one in the class". He suspected too that Augustine was too fearful and unassuming to express his aspirations. Father McGirr asked the question directly: "Augustine, how would you like to be a priest?"

Augustine looked at the priest in open-mouthed wonder;

momentarily he was speechless. "You mean, Father, I can be a priest? I am a Negro, and I can be what you are? Father, do you really think that I could be a priest?"

"I don't see why not", answered Father McGirr with perhaps more conviction than prudence.

"That's what I really want to be, Father, but I didn't think they let a Negro be a priest. Are there any Negro priests, Father?"

"Of course there are Negro priests", said Father McGirr. "There are some in Africa, and if there are none in the United States, then you will be the first one."

Augustine's eyes sparkled with enthusiasm, his face lighted up with a great smile, and his voice trembled with emotion. "Father, I'll go to Africa if I can be a priest. I really want to be a priest as soon as I can."

"You will need to do a great deal of studying, Augustine, and it will take many years, but we will help you through. We will do all we can for you in every way." The pastor talked on and on about a vocation to the priesthood. He explained the prerequisite educational and religious training; then he named several colleges and seminaries, even religious orders that provided such preparation.

Augustine listened intently all the while, wide-eyed and breathless. "But then, right now, Father, I must work in the factory. Mr. Harris pays me five dollars a week. My mother needs my help", said the boy ruefully.

"Well, it won't always be that way, Augustine. A time will come when you can give up the job and devote all your energy toward studies."

Augustine's heart was brimful of happiness. For the next three years he continued to attend winter classes at Saint Peter's School and received special tutoring from Sister Herlinde during the free hours when he was not at the factory.

Every morning, winter and summer, he served Mass at one of three places: Saint Boniface Church; Saint Peter's Church; or Saint Mary's Institute, the convent. In 1872, at the age of eighteen, Augustine completed the final grade at Saint Peter's School and, as recorded in the *Diamond Jubilee History of the Diocese of Springfield*, "graduated with distinction". In this year also, Augustine received the sacrament of confirmation from Bishop Peter J. Baltes, of the Alton (Springfield) diocese.

Father McGirr soon realized that the higher education of Augustine presented a knotty situation. He was not ready for the standard seminary courses; he could not afford college; and—the major problem—he was black. The priest also had misgivings regarding the difficulties Augustine would encounter as a secular priest. In this predicament Father McGirr conferred with Father Schaeffermeyer, his German colleague, who had never lost interest in the youth.

The news that his old protégé wanted to be a priest touched Father Schaeffermeyer deeply. He was sure that he had an absolute and ready solution for the problem. "Ja, ja, we will have him go to Saint Francis Monastery in Teutopolis. The Franciscan Fathers will train him for the holy priesthood", he asserted confidently.

Augustine was elated at the prospect of entering the Franciscan Order. "And right here in Teutopolis, Illinois," he exclaimed, "so close to Quincy and to my home. I will go right away if my mother can get along without my wages", he said to Father McGirr. Mrs. Tolton told the priest and her son that she could manage well enough and that she did not want to put anything in the way of a vocation to the priesthood.

Father McGirr helped Augustine compose his letter of application, and he himself wrote a recommendation for his "parishioner"—a recommendation which, according to those who recorded it, would have gained admittance for the youth to the celestial choir.

Weeks passed by. Two priests and a candidate for the Franciscan Order waited day after day in breathless suspense. Father McGirr wrote a second time; he received an answer and the final verdict: Augustine Tolton did not qualify.

Father Schaeffermeyer and Father McGirr, both sorely disappointed, studied the problem anew. "I will take this case to the bishop", said Father McGirr impetuously.

Augustine was bewildered and disillusioned. He went to and from the tobacco factory each day in stony silence. "If God vonts you to be a priest, you will be von", Father Schaeffermeyer assured him again and again. "Patience, patience, ve must have patience", he said while he redoubled his efforts to encourage the disheartened youth.

Instead of entering the Franciscan Monastery at Teutopolis, Illinois, as a candidate for the priesthood, Augustine donned his tattered denim overalls and returned to the Harris tobacco factory to become a cigar maker. His assignment to the "higher rooms" placed him under the direct supervision of Mr. Patrick McKenny, a friendly and ever-helpful Irishman. This change brought Augustine into the department where first-class cigars were manufactured by hand in the so-called trio system. The work called for skill, dexterity, speed, and coordination on the part of the three workers, who each received nine dollars per week. The materials needed, such as moistened tobacco leaves, filler, wrappers, and binders, were placed at the convenience of the three persons who formed the trio or team and were constantly replenished by other factory hands. The output of each team reached an average of a thousand cigars per day. Augustine said that in his three-year period of service in this department he had handled more than 600,000 cigars—and, he added with a twinkle in his eye, "I never smoked a single one."

One evening as Augustine came home from work, his mother's first words were, "Father Schaeffermeyer is gone; he left the parish and did not tell anyone where he was going. They get a different priest at Saint Boniface."

Augustine was stunned. He dropped his empty lunch pail; the lid fell off, rolled into a corner, and finally rattled into silence. The news was a shock which left him numb. And he was deeply hurt. Father Schaeffermeyer had promised to "see him through", to help him find a way to become a priest. Now he had gone away without a word; he had betrayed him and deserted him in his greatest need. In the dimly lighted room, Augustine sat on a shabby couch and unburdened his grief and his bitter disappointment to his mother. He covered his face with his hands and wept.

Had Father Schaeffermeyer known that Augustine would be so sorely grieved by his unannounced departure, he would undoubtedly have found a way to soften the blow. On the other hand, Augustine, who knew what waiting meant, would have accepted his friend's leaving had he been aware of the fact that after more than twenty years (a longer time than his own lifespan) Father Schaeffermeyer was at last attaining his own goal—to enter the Franciscan Order.

Augustine found solace in the thought that he could rely fully on Father McGirr for counsel and moral support. However, he realized that Father Schaeffermeyer, as dean of the Quincy clergy, exerted a more powerful influence in episcopal circles. Now he had lost a fatherly friend as well as the mainstay of his plans for the priesthood.

Father Schaeffermeyer had from his youth believed that he was being called to be a follower of Saint Francis. But circumstances had brought him to America, where he had now served Saint Boniface Parish for fourteen years. At last he felt free to follow his special call.

With the sanction of Bishop Peter J. Baltes, Father Schaeffermeyer left Saint Boniface parish to follow his "first love"—the Franciscan way of life in a friary. To avert undue demonstration and notoriety, both of which he heartily disliked, he chose not to publicize the time of his departure. The news brought astonishment and conjecture to his parishioners, for they had long regarded their pastor as irremovable and even irreplaceable. But when they later learned the priest's motive they were not surprised in view of his constant devout life and ascetical leanings.

Father Francis A. Ostrop, who had been pastor of Saint Mary's Church in Alton for more than a decade, was appointed to succeed Father Schaeffermeyer. Before he came to Quincy, he received a letter from Father Schaeffermeyer which read in part:

> You will find that I left affairs in order. I think that you will have no difficulty with the accounts dealing with parish finances. The sum indicated under "Education for Priest" which you will find in the records is intended for the education of the Negro boy Augustine Tolton of Saint Peter's parish. Father McGirr of the Irish parish asked that I find a teacher who will prepare the young man for the priesthood. The money is a private donation—not parish funds.
>
> I trust that you will do what you can for the Negro, as he is indeed very worthy. I promised to help him, and now I request you to carry out my promise. I also ask you to take an interest in the boy so far as this lies in your power.

After leaving Quincy, Father Schaeffermeyer went to Kansas to make a spiritual retreat in a Carmelite monastery of which his cousin, Father F. Heiman, was the superior. He spent several months in solitude as preparation for the new way of life he hoped to live—that of the Rule of Saint Francis of Assisi. Early in 1873, he was admitted to the Franciscan friary in Teutopolis. At his profession he took the name Liborius in honor of the fourth-century French saint who had been chosen as patron of Paderborn, Germany.

Meanwhile, Father McGirr redoubled his interest in the candidate for the priesthood. One of the first ways in which he helped Augustine financially was by employing him as part-time custodian of Saint Peter's parish. "You can earn some pocket money and also increase your fund for future schooling. Time will come when you will need all the money you can get your hands on", hinted the priest.

For six winters Augustine had charge of the church, school, and rectory heating plants. Besides that he did as much of the parish chores as his time away from work allowed. The tall lithe youth, swinging a broom or shovel, carrying wood and water, dumping ashes and doing all kinds of other odd jobs, became a familiar sight to the parishioners. Father McGirr referred to the janitor as "one in a million". Augustine usually sang as he worked. Those who heard him were fascinated by the haunting songs so reminiscent of plantation life.

One Saturday morning while Augustine was sweeping the church and thought he was alone, his rich baritone voice rang out in "Jesus, my Lord, my God, my All!" while his brush knocked against the kneelers. Father McGirr, an unseen visitor, slipped out of the church before Augustine had noticed him.

Back at the rectory the priest sat down at his desk in profound thought. His mind raced back and forth between ecclesiastical law and the manner in which these decrees were interpreted and observed. He recalled the qualities that canon law requires of the candidate for the priesthood: integrity, soundness of mind and body, piety, and intelligence. "Augustine has all of these," he mused, "and the Church says nothing against color or race. What's the problem then? How I wish that the heads of seminaries and religious orders of this country could appreciate the caliber of Augustine Tolton. If they did, there would be a stampede to welcome him to their ranks."

Impatiently, Father McGirr rummaged through the papers and letters littering his desk until he found the large envelope with the chancery address in huge handwriting on one corner. It was the reply to a letter he had sent to Bishop Baltes some time earlier. "Find a seminary which will accept a Negro candidate. The diocese will assume the expenses." There was little help in the bishop's letter because Father McGirr had already written to all the seminaries in the country.

His anger mounted as he picked up one letter after another to reread the irrevocable verdicts. A glance at the first page, and he would throw the letter back on the heap. Finally he straightened himself up in his chair, brought his clenched fist down upon the desk with a crash that made the sheaf of "we regrets" and "we're not readys" topple over, half of them sliding down to the floor. "The God of us all", he said with fine Irish fury, "is still the Boss."

6

"WE ARE NOT READY"

The new pastor of Saint Boniface parish made immediate and earnest efforts to fulfill the last request of his predecessor—to help Augustine Tolton on his way to the priesthood. Already in their first meeting, which occurred in the sacristy when Augustine came to serve the early Mass, mutual admiration and trust had been enkindled. Soon Father Ostrop was planning a series of studies for the young man. Not only did he outline the lessons and supply the reading material; he also invited Augustine to come for guidance whenever his job at the tobacco factory allowed.

Almost a year later Father Theodore Wegmann was appointed assistant pastor of Saint Boniface parish. He was young, zealous, and distinguished in those parts for his scholarship. The most sanguine hopes of Father Schaeffermeyer and Father McGirr in behalf of Augustine Tolton were unwittingly realized when Father Ostrop entrusted his further education to Father Wegmann. In long and short unscheduled classes over a period of more than two years—years in which Augustine was a breadwinner and an outcast—Father Wegmann was his devoted teacher, his true counselor, and his loyal friend.

The course of study was patterned on that offered at Saint Francis Solano College, which was conducted by the Franciscan Fathers in Quincy. This was the year 1873, just after the college had received state recognition. In order to

create a classroom atmosphere and to provide competition
and discussion sessions, Father Wegmann organized a class.
Two white students, Clement Johannes and Henry Ording,
who had requested private tutoring, joined Augustine in the
instruction periods, which were usually held during the late
evening hours in the priest's private study. The three students become fast friends, and Father Wegmann's school became—in modern parlance—the first integrated "college"
in Illinois.

Saint Boniface rectory, where Augustine Tolton
was tutored by diocesan priests

Despite the self-sacrificing efforts and intensive teaching
of Father Wegmann, Father Ostrop (who substituted whenever Father Wegmann was engaged elsewhere) and Father
McGirr suffered continuous anxiety regarding Augustine
Tolton. "Sure, we can educate him here, but what about

his seminary training and ordination?" asked Father McGirr again and again. Father Ostrop, too, wondered whether Augustine Tolton, as a secular priest, would be accepted by the whites or by the blacks or even by members of the clergy. "I have written to all the seminaries and religious communities of priests in the country, and they all say about the same thing: 'We are not ready for Negroes'", Father McGirr reported indignantly.

Both priests concluded that a religious community was really the only solution to the problem, but finding a community that would accept a black youth was something else again. The priests discussed the question long and seriously. Father Ostrop recalled the decrees of the Second Plenary Council that had convened in Baltimore in 1866. "The forty-five bishops and archbishops who attended the council came from all parts of the country, North and South, and they faced the Negro question squarely every time it was presented. And, as far as these prelates are concerned, they did take a stand", said Father Ostrop loyally.

"Yes, I know", agreed Father McGirr. "I recall that they demanded from every member that all possible means be implemented for the religious care and instruction of blacks. But what have they achieved? How did they enforce their demands? How did they really improve the situation?"

"Well," answered Father Ostrop pointedly, "it was agreed that anyone neglecting to provide means for the education of all, both black and white, would merit the strongest reproach."

Over and over, the two priests reviewed the moot question of racial equality. Hatreds and prejudices, intensified during the political upheaval known as Reconstruction in the South, were engulfing the whole nation. The priests were aware of the fact that the timidity of individuals and scarcity of manpower and resources in a period of mass Catholic immigration were causing the chances for large-scale conversion of blacks to Catholicism after the Civil War gradually to slip away. Bishop John Lancaster Spalding was prophetic, when even before the Second Plenary Council he expressed concern about the situation: "It is a golden opportunity for reaping a harvest of souls which, if neglected, may not return."

So intense was the southern feeling—and, in many cases, also the northern—against educating blacks that religious communities, some of whose members shared these sentiments, often shied away from the task of integration for fear of alienating white patronage. With hostility continually stirring and acts of violence threatening those who undertook the education of blacks, it is not surprising that the decrees of the Second Plenary Council were ignored in many dioceses.

Father McGirr was fully aware of this situation, but it rankled him beyond endurance that members of the clergy and heads of religious orders were unwilling to brave the consequences that might follow if a black candidate for the priesthood was admitted into their communities. He realized that a black priest might not be accepted in a white world and perhaps not even by his own race, but there was always the possibility that a black priest could do missionary work in a country that did not evaluate him by the color of his skin. "Augustine Tolton is willing to go to Africa," shouted Father McGirr, "but American seminaries and religious communities for priests will not admit him and train him because 'they are not ready for that' ".

Before Father McGirr's zeal could become entangled with his Irish temper, Father Ostrop mentioned that a new religious order for missionary priests had been established in Baltimore. "It seems", he explained, "that these Fathers are from England and were founded to Christianize the emancipated blacks."

Father McGirr, who had been listening in distrustful silence, suddenly jumped to his feet. He thrust a fist into the palm of his hand and exclaimed, "That's the place for Augustine Tolton."

Saint Joseph's Society for Foreign Missions was founded in England by Cardinal Vaughan in 1866. Shortly after the Civil War the then Father Herbert Vaughan had toured America in order to survey the plight of the freed slaves. Wherever he went he was convinced of the necessity for a clergy totally dedicated to the work of Christianization among the blacks. In 1871 Father Vaughan and his four companions, Fathers Cornelius Dowling, James Noonan, Joseph Gore, and Charles Vigeront, went to Rome and asked Pope Pius IX to assign them a mission field among the blacks, either in the United States or in Africa. Since Pope Pius IX had recently approved the decrees of the Second Council of Baltimore appealing for missionary priests to devote themselves to the apostolate of the emancipated slaves, he commissioned the new society to undertake the work under the direction of Archbishop Spalding of Baltimore. When the English missionaries arrived, the archbishop assigned them to the Church of Saint Francis Xavier as a black parish and the site of their first American foundation.

Father McGirr lost no time and spared no effort in pursuing this new possibility. He felt that Father Wegmann, who had instructed Augustine for more than a year, would be able to give an accurate delineation of the applicant's character and schooling. "Write to the pastor of Saint Francis

Xavier Church in Baltimore", he directed. "It will get to the right place by and by; I don't know where the monastery is located."

Obviously Father McGirr envisioned a sizable religious community replete with a seminary and teaching staff, ready to welcome a black applicant even in preference to a white person since their apostolate was solely in the interests of black people. He did not know that the Josephite seminary was still ten years away; that the community consisted of only five members and that these lived in close quarters —a small rented house near the church. From this center, Father McGirr learned later, the five members conducted the parish, catechized the children, and also directed classes for adults. They recruited the scattered blacks of Baltimore, organized initial groups of prospective converts, and performed other regular pastoral duties from early morning till all hours at night. The year 1875, which was the fourth year of the community's existence in America, found the original group still the same in number. Evidence that their efforts were, as one of them expressed it, "bearing fruit" was the letter of application which Father James Noonan, the superior, received and which he shared with his confrères:

> Quincy, Illinois
> April 6th, 1875

Rev. James Noonan
Rector of Saint Francis Xavier Church
Baltimore, Maryland

Dear Sir:

> Having been informed that there exist colleges in London & Baltimore for the purpose of training missionaries for the colored people of the country, thinking that you may have some connection with them, I make bold to apply to you

in behalf of a young man of the African race, who is very desirous of becoming a missionary for the people of his race, and to whom I have been giving instruction for about a year and a half, being requested to do so by his pastor, Reverend Peter McGirr of Saint Peter's Church of this city.

The young man in question is about twenty years old, of an excellent character, and of good talents.

Studying Latin for over a year, he reads Nepos and Caesar without difficulty. Also other branches have not been neglected, and some weeks ago I have begun Greek with him. I am very willing to direct his studies yet for some time, if I can see a prospect for him of attaining the end he aims at, i.e. the sacred priesthood—if I knew of a college that is prepared to admit him afterwards.

Having been directed by our Rt. Rev. Bishop, Peter J. Baltes to apply to the superior of the Missions for Colored people, but not knowing exactly the name, I address myself to you, hoping that you either may be able to give the desired information, or at least be kind enough to forward this letter to the proper person. If further particulars are desired, I would beg leave that you refer to the Rev. Father McGirr of Saint Peter's Church, Quincy, Illinois.

Recommending the young man in question—Augustine Tolton is his name—as well as myself to your good prayers, I have the honor to be

> Your Brother in Xto. Theodore Wegmann
> Assistant priest of Saint Boniface Church
> of Quincy, Adam's County, Illinois

Unlike Father McGirr's collection of "we regret" and "we're not ready" letters, Father Wegmann's appeal brought a response that was not without hope. "Since we do not have a seminary yet and cannot train young men for the priesthood," the superior wrote, "would Mr. Tolton perhaps like to be a catechist? And, if the Fathers at Mill Hill, London accepted him in the English seminary would he be willing later to go as a missionary priest to Borneo . . . ?"

The first question was quickly settled. Augustine wanted to be a priest, not a catechist. Numerous difficulties and problems were associated with the second alternative. Augustine was willing and even eager to go to Borneo (an island in the East Indies) as a missionary priest. But Father McGirr saw the whole matter as a series of entangling obstacles: a huge financial need, racial prejudice, apathy on the part of clerical superiors, double-talk. Even though the letter from Father Noonan showed interest and extended encouragement, the quick-tempered priest read another "we are not ready" between the lines.

There were, of course, ameliorating statements and suggestions. The London headquarters of the order would be consulted, in case the youth chose to be a missionary priest. If the young man wanted to be a catechist in Baltimore, Archbishop Spalding would provide housing because their quarters were already too crowded. But the final counsel, "since Father Wegmann is willing, why not have Augustine continue his studies under the direction of this priest for some time longer?" seemed to be the most feasible procedure to follow for the present.

"In the distant—far too distant—future," mused Father McGirr, "Augustine Tolton will probably be a priest in the African jungles and be indebted to the Saint Joseph Society for Foreign Missions for his good fortune. What about the American Negroes and their clergy—white or black?"

Cigars . . . cigars . . . cigars . . . the janitor work at Saint Peter's Church, and the pleasant rewarding hours of learning in Father Wegmann's study constituted Augustine's life for the next year, his twelfth season as a factory hand for the Harris Tobacco Company. In a letter written to the editor

of the *Saint Joseph Advocate* in 1875, Father Wegmann refers
to this period of his life and his association with Augustine
Tolton: "From May, 1873, to October, 1875," he wrote, "I
instructed the trio—Clement Johannes and Henry Ording
(German students), and Augustine Tolton—in all the leading college branches: Latin, Greek, German, U.S. history,
ancient and modern history, geography, Nepos, Caesar, Ci-
cero, Virgil. Augustine Tolton reads and speaks German flu-
ently."

On one October evening in 1875 a particularly delightful
and challenging session in Father Wegmann's "classrooms"
had taken place. The three students basked in his inspired
interpretation of Greek mythology. They had listened spellbound, asked questions, discussed, and listened again. At
the close of the two-hour period, Father Wegmann failed
to give the usual concise assignments. Instead the instructor
suddenly seemed preoccupied, then gave a kind of general
directive. He showed how further study could be done and
cited sources for further reading.

As the students began to collect their texts and notebooks,
Father Wegmann said in an unsteady voice: "Well, boys, I
suppose there will be no more classes." The three men stood
still in open-mouthed surprise. Trying to regain his compo-
sure, the priest began to fumble in his pockets and finally
produced a letter. "It's from the bishop", he said simply.
"He has appointed me to be pastor of All Saints Parish in
Roselle, Iowa, the diocese of Dubuque."[1]

[1] In 1914, with the division of the diocese of Dubuque, All Saints
Parish in Roselle became a part of the diocese of Sioux City.

7

A DARK INTERLUDE

Peter McGirr and Patrick Dolan, both sons of Irish peasants and staunch Catholics, were born on the same day—June 29, 1833. Peter was named for the Prince of the Apostles, while Patrick received the name of Ireland's patron. The villagers of Fintana, a rural district in Ulster, celebrated the blessed event then and in the subsequent anniversaries in merry-making—singing and dancing, a simple repast, and draining of glasses by the menfolk. The Dolans and McGirrs lived on adjacent small farms. The boys played together; grew up together; and, as everyone knew, were inseparable. Despite this fact they were different in almost every respect—appearance, ability, attitude.

Peter, with a shock of red hair and a face filled to capacity with freckles, was an extrovert—talkative, impulsive as his patron saint, and a man of action. Patrick, dark haired and handsome, was reserved, quiet, indolent, and a dreamer. In school, Peter, with persistent effort and the help of eight brothers and sisters, merited grades just a little below those of Patrick. The only child of a doting mother and an indulgent father, Patrick studied fitfully, rejected every kind of assistance, and walked away with scholastic honors. The two lads served Mass together.

From the time they were small boys Peter and Patrick had been certain they would become priests. By the time they were fifteen years old and had graduated from the district school, their decision was confirmed, not only by the two boys themselves, but by the whole parish. "Sure, Peter and Patrick would make fine priests, they would now," said Mr. McGirr, "but can anybody tell me now where's the money to come from for the education. With the rent higher than ever and me with eight mouths to feed. . . ."

Peter's two older brothers, who had heard the lament of taxes and tithes, mortgages and evictions since they were knee high, chimed in with, "But in America, Father, the wages be higher; jobs there aplenty; we'd be sending you our earnings, we would now."

Time and again the older sons had pleaded parental approval on their plan to leave for America in search of fortune as so many of their friends and acquaintances had done. Finally both father and mother relented, and only because they were now confronted with the problem of Peter's desire to become a priest.

"Nothing must stand in the way," said Mrs. McGirr, "if it is the will of the good Lord to bless us with a priest in the family."

Upon the advice of their parish priest, who agreed to make all the preliminary arrangements, the McGirrs consented to let Peter accompany his brothers to America in order to pursue his studies for the priesthood there. In 1848, after a seven-week ocean voyage the three brothers arrived in New York City. Peter was admitted to Holy Cross College in Worcester, Massachusetts, and his two brothers settled in the same city, where they found well-paying jobs. In less than two years the brothers managed to finance the voyage to America for the other members of their family. The McGirrs found a home in Bloomfield, Illinois, where some of their compatriots had settled earlier.

After completing his classical and philosophical studies, Peter studied theology at the Sulpician Seminary in Montreal, Canada. In 1861 he was ordained by Bishop Juncker for the diocese of Alton, Illinois. A year later, the young priest was appointed pastor of Saint Patrick's Church (later renamed Saint Peter's) of Quincy, and there he was to establish the record of serving in the same pastorate for thirty-five years.

Patrick Dolan's ascent to the priesthood was accomplished with less effort and fewer hardships and sacrifices. He enrolled in Saint Patrick's College of Maynooth, fifteen miles north of Dublin. This college was the training center for the intellectual elite among the diocesan clergy in Ireland. During all his college years and seminary training, Patrick Dolan distinguished himself by his scholarship rather than by his piety. He passed his examinations—classical, philosophical, and theological—commendably and was ordained priest in 1861, the same year as Peter McGirr. Father Dolan's first assignment was a small parish in the episcopal city of Monaghan, diocese of Clogher, located in north central Ireland. His mother died several years after his ordination, and his father, reduced to poverty, lived with relatives.

During the first few years of his ministry, Father Dolan performed his duties faithfully. But as time went on he labored with feigned joy and superficial zeal. Pastoral duties became increasingly burdensome for him. The monotony of daily Mass, the incessant odd-hour sick calls, the insufferable task of hearing confessions, the duty-motivated sermons and instructions weighed on him. He did not fare well with fellow priests, and he had more than one clash with his bishop. Enduring the devastating emptiness of the rectory and the constant loneliness of his study demanded greater stamina and moral strength than he had acquired during his years of training. Because he formed a clique with a group of favorite parishioners, Father Dolan lost the goodwill and confidence of the rest of his people. Since the conduct of his associates was not always above reproach, the priest jeopardized his reputation. The parish teemed with gossip and illwill; petitions for his removal were sent to the bishop.

In the episcopal residence to which he had been summoned, Father Dolan listened to the charges against him. "Father," said the bishop kindly, "let us make a new start. I will assign you to another parish—a smaller one—far away from here. How would you like that, Father Dolan?"

"Your Excellency," answered the priest with real humility, "I will make amends; I will accept the parish you have in mind for me and do my best there. I thank you for the admonition and consideration—and now, Your Excellency, may I have your blessing?"

In his new parish Father Dolan began a period of exemplary activity. The assignment seemed easier; the people were more cooperative and friendly. The priest, apparently enthusiastic and zealous, mingled freely and fraternally with his parishioners. Small groups met at the rectory for parochial transactions. These meetings became more and more frequent and usually closed with a game of cards— for small stakes—and a tinkling of glasses. These "business meetings" eventually became social gatherings of a select group. Little by little Father Dolan fell into his former habits and added a decided addiction for drink. The situation was obviously aggravated by the death of his father. The priest tried to drown his grief and remorse in drinking bouts which lasted several days. The matter had repeatedly been brought to the attention of the chancery, and upon investigation the bishop's worst fears were confirmed.

Again the bishop called for the priest. "Father Dolan,"

he said, trying to hide his disappointment, "let us talk it over again. What can we do about it—how can we help you? You, Father, with your splendid talents, your eloquence, your priestly power and grace? How can we carry out the promises made at your ordination, fulfill the mission to which you were called? The sacrament of Holy Orders equipped you with power and grace—you are another Christ." The bishop, touched by his own words, could go no further.

Father Dolan looked at his ecclesiastical superior with dull, bloodshot eyes. "How understanding and fatherly he is", he thought contritely. It gave him the courage to state his request.

"Your Excellency," he faltered, "since I give you so much trouble and sorrow—since I find myself always a failure, I should like to go away. Let me go to America. Maybe," he added ruefully, "Father McGirr can help me."

Not long after, Father Dolan was en route to America. Through arrangements made by his bishop, he was affiliated with the diocese of Saint Louis, which was then under the jurisdiction of Bishop Peter E. Kenrick, and was assigned to a parish in northeastern Missouri.

In a letter to Father McGirr, which omitted all references to his past tragic experiences in Ireland, Father Dolan described the conditions of his American parish: "The church and rectory are old, in disrepair and very gloomy. The walls of the buildings, both interior and exterior, are discolored, black with dirt and grime; I cannot see through the windows of my room. The whole place is absolutely neglected and filthy. I have no housekeeper, and I don't know where I could find one. I don't know a single soul in this whole state."

Father McGirr stopped reading. "A solution for our problem!" he shouted jubilantly, sailing the letter into the air above his head. Ever since the departure of Father Wegmann several weeks earlier, Father Ostrop and Father McGirr had been trying in vain to procure a teacher for Augustine Tolton or a college which would admit him. He immediately wrote to Father Dolan rejoicing in the good fortune of finding a "scholarly tutor" for Augustine Tolton and also assuring him of the good services Mrs. Tolton would provide as housekeeper for the rectory. "Augustine will do all the work around the church and the sacristy in return for your efforts to give him help in his studies", wrote Father McGirr.

Father Dolan's prompt reply stated that he was satisfied with the arrangements and that he would begin tutoring at once in return for Augustine's work as parish custodian and that he would pay Mrs. Tolton well for her services.

Father McGirr sent for Mrs. Tolton and her son. "You will live in a house near the church", explained the priest after he had told them about the plans he had made. "Father Dolan will pay the rent for you, and he will find a job for Anne", he added with complete assurance.

Mrs. Tolton shuddered when she heard the word "Missouri", but the priest reminded her of the Emancipation Proclamation and the "perfectly safe" conditions in the former slave state.

"Oh, Father McGirr," Augustine chimed in, beaming with pleasure at the good news, "this is another step toward my goal."

At the tobacco factory Augustine had just received another "promotion". He was initiated into the fine art of rolling cigarettes and had already turned these out by the thousands. After his call at the rectory, Augustine informed his employer that he was going to another state to continue his education and that he was giving up his factory job. Mrs. Tolton gave similar notice to her employer in a downtown restaurant, where she had worked as a cook for several years.

Father Dolan received the Toltons with marked courtesy and kindness. He showed them the church, the rectory, and the house he had rented for them. Finally he gave broad directives regarding their duties, and he agreed on a time for Augustine's lessons.

The whole arrangement promised to be satisfactory and altogether successful. The Toltons lost no time cleaning the buildings and the premises. Mrs. Tolton took delight in preparing delectable meals for Father Dolan and his occasional guests. Augustine was fascinated by the priest's lucid explanations of the Greek and Latin classics, as well as by his commentaries on Sacred Scripture.

The young man studied diligently and purposefully, even though the assignments were not always clear and methodical. Then too, there were times when Father Dolan was "engaged elsewhere", and again there were times when Father was "out of town". After a few months the priest began to show signs of boredom and irritation. Much to Augustine's disappointment, he cancelled class hours more and more frequently. The student missed the personal interest and never-failing encouragement which had been vitalizing factors in his earlier educational endeavors.

The Toltons attended Mass also on weekdays when Father Dolan celebrated, but Augustine was crushed when he was told that only white boys could be acolytes. He tried to hide his bitter disappointment and disillusionment from his mother, but she sensed his unhappiness and shared his increasing frustration. Often Augustine would sit glumly in the rectory kitchen where his mother was at work. "Seems like Father Dolan does not like to teach me," he said sadly, "and when I ask questions, he does not answer them."

"I think Father is a sick man", explained his mother with a note of sympathy. "He eats so little, and when he picks up his coffee cup his hand shakes badly."

Mrs. Tolton surmised the priest's weakness. Added to this anxiety was an even greater one: How will this affect Augustine's desire to be a priest? Moreover, the mother was never free from the haunting fear that they all would be kidnapped and sold as slaves. There was proof that this practice still prevailed in Missouri, despite the emancipation.

But then for the next several weeks Father Dolan came regularly to direct Augustine's classes. He was highly nervous but always in exuberant spirits. The youth's trust and confidence were restored. He made very special efforts to learn his lessons well and to please his teacher—or at least not challenge his patience. One evening after he had read and explained a Latin passage in accordance with the instructor's wish, Augustine looked up for approval or for further direction. He saw that Father Dolan had fallen fast asleep.

"There's no use trying", Augustine told his mother. "Here in Missouri I am neither earning nor learning; in Quincy I could at least help you with my job."

Mother and son talked long and confidentially. "With the few chores I now have and with the place all set in order and cleaned up, I could take another job somewhere in town and help us all along. I don't know how to go ahead with my books because Father Dolan does not show me how, and he does not care at all."

"Now, now, Augustine", said his mother loyally. "I am sure Father does care, but he has so much on his mind with the parish and everything. Many times he does not seem to feel well either."

Augustine was not wholly convinced. "Father McGirr

told me there was a chance of my going to England to study. The Saint Joseph Society for Foreign Missions in Mill Hill takes Negroes in. If I earn enough money I can go there to be a priest", he said wistfully.

Consequently, Augustine took an evening job in a local saloon because it was "good paying" and at a time that did not interfere with his lessons or his chores. The proprietor of the place told him sternly that he would have to clean up after the customers left—which usually was after midnight.

Augustine was no stranger to most of the forms of human weakness and evil. Working in this saloon, however, introduced him to a new scene of human degradation. Men and women, too inebriated to walk, were helped out of the place by half-drunks and all too often by tearful wives and mothers. The stench of reeking bodies, alcoholic fumes, and stale tobacco pervaded the whole atmosphere. The room where the all-day and half-night brawls took place was left in a state of incredible disorder. The floor was littered with broken glass, cigar ashes, and playing cards and cluttered with furniture that had been shoved around and overturned.

Besides sweeping and scrubbing the floor, washing tables and chairs, Augustine was told to trim the hanging kerosene lamps, clean the lamp chimneys and reflectors, and shine up the windows of the saloon. Since the liquor storage rooms were locked at night, Augustine was free to work in the main room during the after-closing hours until the doors were opened again for the next day's business. Day after day the heavy-hearted young man walked home in the wee morning hours.

The work, disgusting as it was, did not perturb Augustine. He was deeply grieved, however, at the sight of human beings—men and women, old and young—who frequented the saloon and sacrificed their dignity to wallow there. "How I wish I could help them", he used to say to himself as he cleaned the place. "I wish I could tell them about the goodness of the Lord—save them from the demon of drink, but here I am getting the place ready for them. I cannot go on with this. There must be another way."

One evening at the scheduled time Augustine went to the rectory for his lessons. He wondered whether Father Dolan was home, for he had not seen the priest for several days. With his books clutched under his arm he entered the priest's study; as usual the door was open. Father Dolan, slumped in his armchair, his jaws sagging, was oblivious of Augustine's presence, and the boy's "Good evening, Father" received no response. Several times Augustine called the priest by name; he tugged at his hands and shook his shoulder, but he was unable to rouse the man from his stupor.

The boy stood aghast. He became aware of the peculiar saloon-like odor. Backing out of the room in utter disbelief and sorrow, he went away to get his mother. Together they helped the priest to his feet and gently guided his lurching steps toward his bedroom.

"Write to Father McGirr", said Mrs. Tolton to her son in characteristic Christian compassion. "Tell him that Father Dolan is a sick man who needs help badly."

For some time Father Dolan had been remiss in celebrating daily Mass. Either he came late, or he did not come at all. Parishioners waited until the scheduled hour, and when the priest did not appear they went home. Finally most of them discontinued the practice of attending Mass.

All this while Augustine performed his routine duties at the church and rectory with special care and exactness, despite the fact that his classes had been terminated. He did the loathsome work at the saloon only to help support the family and to save money for his future goal.

Mrs. Tolton's face showed signs of double strain: fear of being kidnapped and fear of Father Dolan's influence on her son's ideals. She waited in painful suspense for the letter of reply from Father McGirr. It was eleven months since they had left Quincy, desperately she wanted to go back.

"Augustine," said Mrs. Tolton excitedly as she hurried out to meet her son, who was just returning home from work, "come quickly! Here is a letter from Father McGirr." The mother waited breathlessly as Augustine scanned the few lines and openly showed her relief and satisfaction when he said, "Father McGirr says for us to come back to Quincy."

"The goodness of the Lord", said Mrs. Tolton softly. Then she looked long and quizzically at her son. Augustine responded in complete understanding and trust. "Mother," he said fervently, "more than ever, I want to be a priest."

8

FRANCISCAN OVERTURES

The Franciscan friary at Teutopolis, Illinois, closed its doors to Augustine Tolton when, in 1872, he applied for admission. And yet, Augustine always gave credit to a German priest of this order for opening the way to his career.

To give an adequate account of the influence and assistance this religious community exerted upon the aspiring candidate to the priesthood, it is necessary to trace Franciscan beginnings in Quincy and to point out the individual characters and the step-by-step events responsible for Augustine Tolton's ultimate victory.

The year 1858 marks the initial contact of the Franciscan Fathers with Quincy, Illinois. At that time Father Herman Schaeffermeyer, pastor of Saint Boniface Church, requested clerical assistance from Saint Francis Friary, Teutopolis, because his rapidly growing parish could no longer be served adequately by one priest. His request was granted during the 1859 Easter season. Father Capistran Zwinge arrived and was the first Franciscan to exercise the priestly ministry in Quincy. The subsequent fruitful services of these friars included a short-lived but highly significant apostolate to blacks.

During the period that Father Capistran was his guest in the parish rectory, Father Schaeffermeyer expressed the wish that a second German parish be established in the city, and this under the auspices of the Franciscan Fathers. The plans were formulated and discussed with other members of the order, who took turns assisting at Saint Boniface Church during the next two years. Among them were these memorable pioneers: Father Servace Altmicks, Father Herbert Hoffmann, Father Maurice Klostermann, Father Raynerius Dickneite, and Father Bernardin Hermann. The concurrence of episcopal approval, the consent of Father Provincial Janknecht, and the Christian Borstadt donation,[1] consisting of an entire city block, resulted in the first Franciscan establishment in Quincy, Saint Francis Solano Church and Friary.

Within the next decade Saint Mary's Hospital, staffed by Sisters of Saint Francis; Saint Antonius Church; and Saint Francis Solano College (later Quincy College) came into existence in the wake of Father Schaeffermeyer's initiative. As the cornerstone was being laid for each one of these foundations—a ceremony in which he as vicar general of the diocese and head of the Quincy deanery was asked to officiate—Father Schaeffermeyer was unaware of the fact that he was laying steppingstones for his protégé, Augustine Tolton.

Both Father McGirr and Father Ostrop welcomed the Toltons warmly when they returned to Quincy after the unhappy episode in Missouri. Their interest in Augustine doubled as they noticed his renewed determination.

"I must work harder; I must get a better job", he told Father Ostrop—almost in a state of panic one morning after

[1] Mr. Christian Borstadt was a member of Saint Boniface parish and owner of considerable property in Quincy. He felt particularly indebted to the sons of Saint Francis, for, when he was still a traveling apprentice in Germany, he contracted a deathly illness in the city of Fulda. The Franciscans residing there took him into their friary until he regained his health. He promised that if he ever had a chance to help the Franciscans he would gladly do so.

serving an early Mass at Saint Boniface. "I must earn and save money so that I can go to England or any other place that will let me in so that I can get seminary training and be ordained."

The priest noticed how desperately Augustine clung to the only and remote chance he had been offered—to join the Saint Joseph's Society in Mill Hill, where he could be trained for missionary work in Africa, Borneo, or possibly the United States. Father Ostrop remembered that the Josephite superior in Baltimore, Father Noonan, had explained the fact that they were establishing a foundation for the black apostolate but that they had no seminary in this country. Father Noonan had stated further that a seminary would be opened as soon as possible for the training of American candidates. Time and again Augustine rehearsed the possibility of going to England, and he clung to this hope.

The shops at the Harris tobacco factory had just been closed for the season when the Toltons returned from Missouri. Mrs. Tolton was promptly rehired by her former employer; Augustine found work at the J. L. Kreitz Sattlergeschäft (a saddle factory). He was forced to settle for a low-paying job be cause he lacked the necessary experience and skills.

"Mr. Kreitz says I can learn on the job", Augustine informed his mother. "He is having one of the men show me how to cut out the stuff for horse collars. We have to use sharp knives and heavy scissors to slit the leather; one of the other men will teach me how to put it together. After I learn how to make those horse collars and saddles, I'll get much better pay. It will take a while before I can do this the right way and also be fast about it."

Father McGirr asked Augustine to continue his work as

parish custodian. Once again the familiar plantation songs were heard on and around the premises of Saint Peter's Church, and everyone was glad that Augustine was back.

"What about your schooling, Augustine?" asked Father Ostrop as he met the youth on his way to work. "Don't you think you ought to go on with your studies?"

Augustine's face brightened. "Oh, I hope I can, Father. I want to learn more and more. Do you know of anyone who will be my teacher?"

"Yes, I do", answered the priest warmly. "I talked with Father Reinhart today. He was assistant priest here in Father Schaeffermeyer's time. Father Reinhart told me today that he would be glad to be your teacher if you would come to his study at Saint Mary's Hospital. He is the chaplain there now. Just take your books and tell him I sent you. Sister Perpetua, the superior at the hospital, will show you where to go."

The staff and patients at the hospital soon noticed the daily coming and going of the tall black student with a pack of books under his arm. "He takes classes from Father Reinhart", they told visitors and incoming patients. "He is going to be a priest and go to Africa or someplace; that is what he told Sister Perpetua."

Father Reinhart was a highly qualified, understanding, and sympathetic teacher. As early as 1865 Father Schaeffermeyer had recommended him as pastor of the newly established Saint Mary's Church, located on Seventh and Adams Streets, about a mile south of Saint Boniface. The young priest was capable and energetic and immediately assumed full responsibility. The unremitting work and strain associated with the building of a church had a devastating effect upon the priest's health. He had exerted himself to the fullest extent and even beyond his strength. By the time Saint Mary's Church was completed, Father Reinhart's vitality was shattered; it was impossible for him to accept the pastorate. He was admitted to Saint Mary's Hospital as a patient. In 1876, when his health was sufficiently restored, he was appointed chaplain of the same hospital.

Then, several months after Augustine began his studies under his direction, Father Reinhart was assigned assistant pastor at Saint Boniface. Consequently, Augustine's lessons were again conducted in the same study where he had received instruction in Father Wegmann's three-student class, although he was now the sole pupil of Father Reinhart.

One evening in the fall of 1877, Augustine, whistling a livelier tune than usual, bounded up the steps leading to the rectory. "I have a new job, Father", he announced as he met Father Ostrop at the door. "It's at Durholt and Company, a soda firm. Mr. John Flynn is the manager there, and he said he would take me on right away. And I get twelve dollars a week."

"Good news!" exclaimed the priest heartily. "That's better than you were getting at the tobacco factory."

"Oh, yes, Father, and it is nearly twice as much as I was making on horse collars."

Father Ostrop nodded approval and continued to look intently at the youth as, loaded with books, he made his way to Father Reinhart's study. "That fine lad is not supposed to be working in a tobacco factory, a horse collar factory, or any other factory. He should be in a seminary", he said to himself as he walked away.

Everyone who knew Augustine saw a new light in his eyes and a more hopeful expression on his face and in his whole attitude. "My earnings are growing bigger and bigger", he told Father McGirr as he was handed his monthly paycheck. "Some day I will have enough to go away to a seminary. I wish I could go right now. Looks like I am going altogether too slow."

At his first opportunity Father McGirr conferred again with Father Ostrop. "We must do something for him, Father, and we must do something before you leave Quincy. You are leaving us, and I just heard that Father Reinhart is also transferred. Do you think, Father, that the Franciscans at Saint Francis College will admit a Negro?"

"Why, yes, I think they will. As a matter of fact," said Father Ostrop, "I did talk with the rector, Father Anselm Mueller, and he said they would gladly accept Augustine, but he doubts whether they will offer courses advanced enough for him. He thinks that after all the tutoring Augustine has had from Father Wegmann and Father Reinhart, they would have to appoint special teachers for him and organize more advanced courses. Father Anselm seemed willing to do this."

Saint Francis College, which was founded in 1860, had from its beginning experienced serious difficulties and problems. Although there were competent teachers—religious and lay—there were no college-level students. The mental caliber of some of the young men who enrolled was so elementary that they could not even be classed as high-school pupils. The Franciscan faculty faced the situation and solved the problem by simply converting the proposed college into a high school and even adding elementary-grade subjects to the curriculum. The institution became known as a preparatory school and served that purpose for several years. Then in 1870, when Father Janknecht, the provincial superior, visited Quincy, he ordered the establishment of an institution of higher learning. The college as such opened in 1871 and two years later received the legal charter of the State of Illinois authorizing it to confer academic degrees. Through the untiring efforts of the rector, Father Anselm Mueller, and

Saint Francis Solano College, Quincy

the other faculty members, the curriculum was enlarged so that it comprised four years of high school and two years of junior college. Courses in philosophy were not offered until 1879.

Father Michael Richardt, O.F.M.

Augustine Tolton was registered at Saint Francis College in 1878, immediately after Father Reinhart left Quincy. He was accepted as a special student and granted the privilege of private instruction. The courses he had pursued earlier were appraised and instructors assigned to direct further study and to fill the gaps in his academic background. Between them Father Engelbert Gey, O.F.M., and Father Francis Albers, O.F.M., taught Augustine mathematics, science, and literature.

The appointment of a third teacher, Father Michael Richardt, O.F.M., bears the unmistakable stamp of Divine Providence. As far back as 1859 Father Schaeffermeyer had unwittingly laid the foundation for this event in the life of

Augustine Tolton. In that year, as ecclesiastical dean, Father Schaeffermeyer had been assured that the Franciscan priests would minister in Quincy and had forthwith planned Saint Antonius Church in a rural area five miles from the city. The parish was composed of scattered German families and was served by priests from Saint Francis Friary. In 1877 Father Richardt was appointed pastor of this parish. He traveled to and from Saint Antonius Church on horseback every Saturday and Sunday. A second task was now given to him by his superior: instructing Augustine in theology and philosophy. Father Richardt, "the missionary teacher", and the two other priests—teachers from the college—scheduled classes at hours when the young breadwinner was not required to work.

Late in the evening or early in the morning, Augustine Tolton was a familiar figure in Quincy as he hurried to and from work or strode in and out of Saint Francis College. He knew all the fathers and brothers at the friary. "They treat me like a member of the community," he told his mother, "and every one of them calls me Gus." Then one day he met his old friend, Father Schaeffermeyer, now Father Liborius of the Franciscan Order. The conversation that followed the joyful reunion was long and serious. "If God vonts you to be a priest, you vill be von", insisted Father Liborius, in his usual tone of confidence. And Augustine, though he remembered that his mentor had said this many times before, came away with renewed courage and hope.

The other students at Saint Francis College mingled freely with Augustine; they admired his diligence and constant cheerfulness; they were charmed by his unfailing wit. It was common knowledge that he was preparing for the priesthood and that he was saving his money to pay for a seminary training.

When Father Richardt heard about Augustine's intentions of going away to study, he asked the question directly: "Where do you intend to go, Augustine?"

"To the Saint Joseph's Society in Mill Hill, England, Father", said Augustine with full conviction.

"What do you know about this society? And how do you know they will admit you?" the priest questioned further.

Augustine was slightly surprised that Father Michael Richardt did not know about the Saint Joseph's Society.

"Well, Father," he explained, "Father Wegmann wrote to the fathers of that society about me. They have a place here in America at Baltimore. They work there just for Negroes. The name of their church is Saint Francis Xavier, and the superior is Father Noonan. They would have taken me in if I would have been a catechist, but I want to be a priest. Because they have no seminary yet I have to go to England to study. The main house of the society is in Mill Hill, and that is where the seminary is."

Father Michael was impressed by the boy's earnestness and determination. His account of the work done by the Saint Joseph Society also affected him deeply. "I wish we could do something for the Negroes here in Quincy", he said feelingly. "There are so many young people and children here who would make good Catholics."

Augustine was all aglow. "Father Noonan did say that I could be a catechist—teach religion and prayers to black children in Baltimore. Why couldn't I be a catechist here in Quincy on Sundays?"

An idea which Father Richardt had nurtured for a long time suddenly took shape. "Why, yes," he said enthusiastically, "why don't we do something for the children right here in Quincy?"

"There are lots and lots of children who would come to

Sunday School if we had one", said Augustine confidently. "I know where most of the Catholic children live. But— where could we have the classes?"

Father Richardt had the answer. "You know that empty old church building at Seventh and Jersey—the old Protestant church? It belongs to Saint Boniface parish; they bought it from the German Lutherans and used it for a school before they built the new one. They are not using it for anything now. I'm going to find out if they'll let us have it for a Sunday School."

9

THE LAY APOSTLE

In the year 1866, when Father Schaeffermeyer was pastor of Saint Boniface's parish, a small Protestant church two blocks away had been purchased for seven thousand dollars. The building was used as a parochial school addition because the original school—combined sisters' convent and classrooms—was no longer adequate. With the erection of a new school in 1875, during the pastorate of Father Francis Ostrop, the old church building was abandoned. When Father John Janssen became pastor in 1877, it had stood vacant for more than two years.

Father Janssen, who was also vicar general of the diocese, took an immediate and active interest in Father Richardt's Sunday School project. He as well as his colleagues were deeply concerned about work among the blacks in Quincy. They had seen new prejudices and more hostile attitudes on the part of the whites emerge as the city grew. The priests regarded the situation with dismay and grave concern, especially as it affected black Catholicism.

Before and during the Civil War, the river town of Quincy was the terminus of several underground railroads, including the Muldew Eastern Road. Thus thousands of blacks came to Quincy. Some of them found homes and the means of earning a living; others eventually moved to northern cities, where they were shunted off into ghettos. Some counties and many towns passed stringent laws forbidding Negro settlements or even overnight stops in certain localities. At its peak the black population of Quincy probably reached three thousand. During the period of civil strife and reconstruction the number fluctuated between several hundred and a few thousand.

Among the fugitives or refugees were some baptized Catholics, and most of these first came to Saint Peter's Church. Father McGirr, the pastor, welcomed them sincerely and invited them to become permanent members of his parish. Father Schaeffermeyer and succeeding pastors of Saint Boniface parish also encouraged the blacks to attend divine worship. Some of the white Catholics of both parishes, however, were ill disposed and even antagonistic toward black people. In subtle ways and studied attitudes, probably born of guilt-laden hatred, prejudiced white parishioners flaunted their supposed superiority and displayed marked resentment toward the presence of black worshipers. The result—a dwindling attendance—saddened the priests; they expended every effort to avert further loss of membership. In season and out of season, the pastors and their assistants pointed out the Gospel messages—definitive words of Christ relevant to fraternal love: As long as you did it to the least of my brethren you did it to me . . . He who says that he loves God and hates his neighbor, the same is a liar; and the shattering injunction "leave thy gift at the altar and go first and be reconciled to thy brother". Despite these pastoral exhortations and scriptural warnings, both parishes suffered an almost total alienation of black members.

In the light of these facts, it is easy to understand why Father Janssen was so ready to give up the vacant building and genuinely glad that it was being used in a worthy cause. With the help of his parishioners he set the place in order and provided the necessary furnishings and equipment. He charged the custodian with the duty of heating, cleaning, and maintaining the building.

But Augustine was impatient to begin. He continued to remind Father Richardt of the Sunday School they had planned earlier.

"As soon as you have a place for us, Father, I'll bring the children around", said Augustine with ill-concealed anxiety.

"Well, you see, Augustine," explained the priest, "Father Janssen is new here. I had to give him time to get acquainted with his parish before I asked him for that vacant church. But we could start teaching already. Why don't we begin the classes in Saint Francis Parochial School? Father Anselm, my superior, suggested that to me."

Augustine was elated. True to his word, he canvassed the ghetto for children of Catholic families. The following Sunday afternoon he brought the first group—five girls and seven boys—to the parish school. From the beginning, this arrangement was understood as temporary.

"We may soon have a Sunday School of our own", Augustine told the children hopefully. "Then you won't need to walk so far."

When Father Michael Richardt entered the classroom, all the children eyed him with obvious surprise and awe; they stared incredulously at his brown robe and his bare feet. As the priest moved forward, the smaller ones fled from their seats and in sheer panic crowded around Augustine, clutching his hands or his jacket. Augustine coaxed them back to their places and told them to look at the holy pictures which Father Richardt distributed. The priest began to explain each representation of Christ, Mary, and the saints. After that he tried to tell them some Bible stories. When the session ended, all the children rushed out of the room and scampered down the street as fast as their spindly legs could carry them.

"There will be more children here next Sunday," said Augustine, picking up the holy pictures which the excited children had dropped, "and they won't be so scared after they come a few times."

"It's rather uphill work," admitted the priest, mopping his brow with a large red handkerchief, "and it seems they can't read a single word—I mean the older ones."

"Oh, no, Father, they can't read", replied Augustine. "They have never been to school, and their parents haven't either. The children will learn by watching and listening."

"Watching and listening", repeated Father Richardt. "What do you mean?"

"Well, Father," explained the youth, "the children must hear us say the prayers and the catechism and watch us do things like going to church and see how Mass is celebrated and how we do things in church. They must watch us receive Holy Communion and go to confession. They have to hear the priest read the Epistles and Gospels and listen to the sermons and instructions. That is the way they will learn. That is the way I learned." Augustine recalled the many times he had "celebrated Mass" for his alley playmates and how they had participated as Mass servers, choir, congregation, and communicants. (A true Montessorian!)

Every Sunday afternoon as long as the school was in existence and while he was in Quincy, Augustine taught the small children in the rear of the thirty-six-foot by seventy-foot room, while the priest instructed the older group in the front area.

From the outset, Sister Herlinde Sick, longtime teacher at Saint Peter's School, took wholehearted interest in the project. Ever since Augustine had been her pupil she had kept in touch with him and encouraged him in his aspiration toward the priesthood. Sister Herlinde was edified when the Sunday School venture materialized and the room filled with black children who came to learn about God; she was especially pleased that Augustine had recruited them and that he continued to do so. In fact, she was firmly convinced that the undertaking would not have been possible without the influence and zeal of Augustine Tolton—a lay apostle.

After a few months of catechizing, Father Richardt and Augustine reached the conclusion that the children must be taught to read and write. "They must learn that, and we must teach them," said the priest, "but how much can we accomplish with one session a week? That is as much time as I can spare from all the other duties piled on me."

"I would come and help in whatever way I can if we had a regular school," mused Augustine, "but I can't give up my job now because I must earn and save money so that I can study for the priesthood."

Augustine took the problem to Sister Herlinde. "We will begin to look into the matter", said the sister encouragingly —although she already had an answer in mind. At his first opportunity Augustine confided to Father Richardt that he thought Sister Herlinde would be willing to teach in the one-room Negro school if she were assigned by her superior.

There was happy excitement and unusual merriment in Saint Mary's Institute. All the School Sisters of Notre Dame who lived there rejoiced with Sister Herlinde, who had received an answer to her letter of request directed to the mother general of her community. She was granted what she called a "promotion". All the sisters were aware of Sister Herlinde's interest in black children and her concern for the whole race. The approval of Mother Mary Caroline terminated an eleven-year term of service at Saint Peter's School and commissioned Sister Herlinde to take charge of the school for black children, commonly designated as Saint Joseph's. Under this arrangement Father Richardt continued to teach religion classes every Sunday, and, as Sister Herlinde stated, "Augustine kept on bringing in more and more children and helped them with their prayers and catechism."

An account of the lowly origin of Saint Joseph's School is given by a contemporary writer, Father Theodore Bruener, in his book, *Kirchengeschichte Quincy's*, published in 1887.

The opening occurred on October 21, 1877, in a so-called Sunday School [it read in German]. The response was quite satisfactory, and during the following winter the enrollment increased to such an extent that the establishment of a day school was considered.

Mother Mary Caroline, superior general of the School Sisters of Notre Dame, Milwaukee, Wisconsin, was wholeheartedly in favor of the plan and was willing to make personal sacrifices. She appointed a sister to teach the school, cancelling the usual remuneration. The day school, to be exact, opened on February 11, 1878, with twenty-one pupils, and, in the course of the year, the number reached sixty. No wonder that the Protestants took sharp notice of the new enterprise designed to propagate the Catholic faith. On April 22, 1878, seven children of Saint Joseph's School were baptized. This occasioned a protest meeting on the part of Methodists and Baptists against the Catholics, and they adopted the unanimous resolution to send all their children to the public school. They employed every means possible to hinder the children from going to the Catholic school. Nevertheless Saint Joseph's School continued and progressed even though some of the baptized Catholics and others discontinued their attendance: new pupils came in the places of those who were lured away.

These same facts are reiterated amid others included in a letter of Father Richardt, dated March 12, 1887, and addressed to the Josephite Fathers of Baltimore:

> Notwithstanding the indignation and opposition meetings, we soon had many children and within the next year, with the grace of God, had the happiness of solemnizing several times, baptisms, Communions, and marriages.

The silent, unobtrusive activity of Augustine Tolton was largely responsible for the success of the apostolate to the blacks of Quincy. Both he and his mother were tireless in their efforts to reinstate members of their race in the Church and to encourage others to study the Catholic religion. They made contacts among their fellow laborers, on the streets while going to and from work as well as in visits to hovels and tenement houses of the segregated areas. Augustine found some of the shacks and rooming houses crawling with vermin and a natural setting for drunkenness and its attendant evils. Many of these conditions shocked him but at the same time aroused his compassion and fired his zeal.

"Many of these people are Catholic", thought Augustine. "If they are sinners, they should have a chance to be helped back to God. They could go to the sacraments and get their lives straightened out. I wish I were a priest and could do something for them."

In connection with his apostolic work Augustine encountered many "victims of drink". Kindly and sympathetically he encouraged them to join the Temperance Society established by Father McGirr. He counseled especially young people to become members of the society, and for the sake of good example he himself joined. As Father Wegmann wrote to the Josephite Fathers in the same letter in which he recommended Augustine for their society, "Augustine was always a prominent member of the Temperance Society (teetotal abstinence) of Saint Peter's Congregation. I remember that Augustine told me that he never tried liquors of any kind, that he didn't even know how liquors tasted."

In the hope of saving his fellowmen, Augustine frequented the city's drinking places, where white and black inebriates intermingled in the daily and nightly bouts and brawls. He listened patiently, often far into the night, to a tangled tale of woe drawled out by a bleary-eyed victim of drink. Augustine was convinced that this attention— the first step in the long, hard battle against drunkenness —would eventually pay off. He understood the problems and temptations of his race; he knew the underlying causes of the weakness and degradation in which many were steeped. With all his heart he deplored the lack of spiritual guidance and opportunities for rehabilitation open to untutored and downtrodden blacks. Yet, he could understand why some white people were hostile, why many Catholics were indifferent, and why those in positions of authority in the Church sometimes vacillated.

Even though many of Augustine's "converts" were temporary and his work looked useless by any earthly standards, he believed that any drunkard who had attended even one meeting of the Temperance Society had taken a step forward; that such a one would benefit by making contact with persons who cared; that he was a little stronger after he became the member of a society that did not exclude blacks. And whenever he succeeded in getting a drunkard to have a "talk" with Father McGirr, he felt quite certain that a conversion had been effected.

Augustine's success as a lay apostle resulted for the most

part from his own day-after-day good example. "He was always a good boy," Father Wegmann wrote to the Josephites, "a good Christian, and there is no doubt that he will live and die a good, faithful—not to say, saintly priest." Yet he was becoming more and more aware of the inadequacy of his efforts. "If I were a priest, I could do so much more for our people", he told his mother again and again. "We should have a church for the Negroes—a church we could call our own. If I were a priest, I could bring them forgiveness and grace and strength. I could help people to become better."

It was common knowledge that Augustine rarely passed a Catholic Church without slipping inside. Father McGirr spoke of the way in which Augustine brought his problems to the right place: "Many a time I caught him in the church on a Sunday afternoon or late evening—a solitary adorer."

From the very outset Father Richardt was impressed by the intelligence, determination, and genuine piety of his student. Years later, after Father Richardt had served two terms as provincial superior of his order, he recalled Augustine's part in the development of Saint Joseph's parish. "I could not have accomplished a thing without his help," he told his confreres, "because I was wholly unacquainted with Negroes; they would not have come without an intermediary. Augustine was instrumental in getting the children to attend Sunday School and the day school; later he encouraged adults to come also, and from this nucleus a parish emerged. In fact Augustine Tolton was an energizing force not only for his race but for me as well."

After Augustine had passed his twenty-fourth birthday, Father Richardt noticed a certain anxiety and restlessness in his bearing—the mounting desires, unspoken hopes, and unfulfilled yearning. "Augustine has done all he can for his people here in Quincy," said Father Richardt to Father Mc-Girr, "and we must soon do something for him; he is determined to study for the priesthood."

The two priests conferred long and seriously—far into the night. "The lay apostle", they finally agreed, "must be given the opportunity to become an ordained apostle—a priest."

10

THE LESSON

One evening the lanky young man whom everyone recognized as Father Richardt's special student entered the classroom for the regular period of instruction. He laid his armful of texts and sundry notebooks on the desk and jerked a pencil from his pocket. After the usual pleasantries ending in hearty laughter, teacher and pupil settled down for the study of philosophy.

"Well, Augustine, now that you have read the *Summa Theologica* on the virtue of justice," said Father Richardt by way of introduction, "let's get on with the various aspects of this cardinal virtue. Under which divisions does Saint Thomas treat justice?"

"Commutative justice, distributive justice, and legal justice", recited Augustine perfunctorily, apparently unaware of the profound implications and ramifications involved in these categories.

The apathetic attitude with which his student faced that day's lesson surprised the priest, but it added an incentive to explain the Thomistic preachings of justice and to clarify it with examples relevant to everyday living. Father Richardt held on to the sheet of paper upon which he had made broad outlines. Undecipherable words appeared in the margins and under the three division heads that Augustine had named. The priest glanced momentarily at the paper, letting his eyes race up and down the columns of factual and illustrative information intended to support his instruction.

"Now then," the lector began, *"justice is the habit residing in the will, prompting that power constantly to render unto everyone his due. The fundamental notion of justice is some sort of equality. Justice is all virtue whatsoever, inasmuch as it bears upon another person than him who practices it."* With a clenched fist pounding the top of the desk, Father Richardt emphasized each word of the final statement. *"It means to give to every man his due."*

The priest noticed the faraway look in Augustine's eyes —a look portending challenge or even defiance concerning the quoted passage. "A little complicated, is it?" he asked.

"Every man his due", echoed Augustine, evading the question. At that moment the instructor's crumpled paper with the lesson outlines slithered unnoticed to the floor and lay face upward between the two men. Its profound content of theory and theology gave way to the actual and the practical.

"Certainly," said the priest, "justice means to give to every man his due."

"Just what is every man's due?" asked the youth timidly.

"Why, Augustine," answered the priest patiently, "you remember that. Every man is entitled to life, to liberty, and to the pursuit of happiness. These so-called natural rights are so necessary and so sacred that all other persons than the one in whom they reside are morally restrained from interfering with them."

The flicker of a smile brightened Augustine's face; it encouraged the instructor to make further precisions.

"It is the duty of every person to respect the rights of every other person. The ultimate source of man's natural rights are found in the will and reason of God, who has decreed that all men shall pursue self-perfection and that they shall not arbitrarily deprive one another of the means essential to this purpose.''

"Well, Father," began Augustine hesitatingly, "Negroes, then, at least in America, have not been treated with justice, or aren't Negroes counted as people?"

"Of course, Negroes are people!" shouted the priest indignantly. "Every person, white or black, is endowed with God-given rights which no man, system of government, or state may violate. Anyone who does infringe upon the rights of others incurs guilt—a guilt commensurate with the degrees of violation. There are major and minor ways in which one person can inflict an injustice upon another or a state upon another state. Can you give an example of this, Augustine?"

"Slavery", stated the youth with conviction. "This system was supported by the state. Under it people were often deprived of life—their liberty was taken away—and they had no chance for happiness."

Father Richardt's slow nod prompted Augustine to continue: "Father, there are Negroes right here in Quincy who have watched an overseer beat a slave to death. They know that many died of inhuman treatment, hard labor, or starvation. Everyone knows that black slaves were put to death because of old age or incurable disease, that crippled or sickly infants were killed outright."

Aroused by his own recital of these wrongs, Augustine raised his voice almost to a shout as he went on: "The laws against murder were never enforced in cases dealing with Negroes. Many white people in the South—and elsewhere too—treated the slaves like animals. In fact, the Negroes were accounted even lower than beasts."

"Yes, yes, Augustine", interrupted the priest as he noted

the youth's rising passion. "But not all slave owners were murderers. The institution of slavery, undesirable as it was, has at times been condoned under the plea that masters bought slaves for the sole purpose of securing labor. They did not actually own the slaves as persons since they could not purchase the intellect and will of anyone—these remain under the control of every person, or every slave, making each one responsible for his voluntary acts."

"I understand that," said Augustine slowly, "but what about the cases where life was actually taken? Or the instances in the past, or right now in the present, when the life of a Negro is shortened by ill treatment or neglect or abuse? How can this injustice be tolerated? These wrongs be righted?"

"Some wrongs cannot be righted", asserted Father Richardt. "Life cannot be restored to a person, but the murderer can make restitution by voluntary acts of penance if God gives him this grace. In other words, the killer of another person is absolutely at the mercy of an all-just God."

"Father, you mentioned that a master did not actually own a slave's will and intellect when he acquired a slave. What chances did these slaves have to develop their wills and minds? Look at the thousands of persons who are illiterate, mentally and morally stunted. Even today, isn't the treatment given Negroes an enormous injustice? Isn't it a matter of some human beings violating the rights of other human beings?"

Father Richardt nodded sadly.

"I am thinking of the thousands, in fact, millions of slaves," Augustine persisted, "who lived in America after they were kidnapped from Africa or sold at auction. All this came to my mind when I studied Saint Thomas' definition of justice. Generation after generation of white people not only deprived Negro slaves of mental and moral development, but they squelched their natural potential by shackling them to intolerable labor, flogging them mercilessly, and subjecting them to inhuman cruelties.''

The student looked up and noticed the priest staring helplessly into space. "Father," he said in a low voice, "I know what I am talking about. I know about slavery."

For a while both men sat in silence. Then Augustine went on, "And you know, Father Richardt, that it still is the belief and the practice of many white Americans that the Negro must be completely subjected and therefore kept completely illiterate. Oh, tell me, where does justice come in? Giving every man his due? Why are such wrongs permitted? How can such things be set aright?"

Father Richardt looked glumly at the crumpled sheet on the floor.

"Don't lose courage, Augustine. God is still in heaven", he said. "He knows how to help a race which has been outraged and deprived of human dignity and self-respect."

"Deprived of human dignity and self-respect?" exclaimed Augustine who had risen to his feet and was pacing back and forth. "That defines it exactly." His pencil slipped from his fingers and rolled onto the sheet of paper containing the instructor's outlines.

"Oh, Father," he said in a voice charged with emotion, "I cannot tell you how deeply I feel for my race. We have lost contact with human beings. We are only a class—a class of dehumanized, brutalized, depersonalized beings. Why are we looked upon as a population of freaks with no natural rights? What is the use of studying about justice? Why don't we do something about it?" he pleaded. "I see it all along, Father. I see it right here in Quincy. Just look at the many Negroes driven to thievery, to rape, to drink—mainly as a result of degradation and lack of responsibility. How can a dehumanized person have responsibility? And Father, don't we all know about the slave master's common practice of selling his slaves' own offspring 'down the river'?"

Father Richardt listened to the all-too-well-known facts. He rose, came from his place behind the desk, and gently grasped the arm of the excited student; he led him back to his chair saying, "You must be calm and patient, Augustine. You and I do not understand the inscrutable ways of God. A time will come when your people will be helped—that is, reinstated."

"But, Father Richardt," interrupted Augustine in a sub- dued tone, "each one of us has just one life to live, and we can't wait. We are ready now to receive justice and equality, opportunity, and religion. Why are we too often given the lowest jobs, the poorest pay, the worst homes, and the most unsanitary living conditions? Why can't we go to Catholic schools and churches without being insulted? Why do some people despise us, hate us, call us niggers, bastards, coons? Why are we isolated like lepers, segregated, shoved aside, kicked, spit upon? This happens all over the country wher- ever Negroes try to settle, and Father, it happens right here in Quincy. Just what have we done to be treated like this? Father Richardt, can you tell me why white people hate us?"

The priest spoke with a voice laden with sorrow. Well, Augustine, greater minds than mine have been unable to give the real and sole motive for the white man's ill will and prejudice. I believe it is based on fear—a fear which stems from guilt. White people know that the Negro has been wronged in slavery days as well as since the emancipa- tion and that by this mistreatment they have incited them to revenge. Isn't this quite natural? Therefore a latent fear exists, and it continues to harass the guilty race—and fear engenders hatred. Do you think this may be one reason, Augustine?"

The student had no answer.

"Of course", continued the priest, "there are those who believe that Negroes are inferior, not capable of leadership or intellectual pursuits. Others again are afraid the blacks will take the white man's jobs in the economic world. Therefore they give them low-paying work to keep him from becoming rich and powerful and thus endangering white supremacy. To ward off this possibility, many white people persist in making the Negro subservient—'keep him in his place', as the saying goes. This vicious attitude and practice are perpetuated as parents warn their children against all blacks and, from their earliest years, instill in their minds the same fear and hatred which they themselves inherited from their forebears."

Augustine sat in gloomy silence as the priest talked on.

"Some interpreters base hatred for the Negro on race differences. Such an attitude, I believe, may cause unconcern or neglect, maybe the urge to repress or downgrade the race, but it would scarcely be accompanied by downright hatred. Hatred is enkindled and nourished by the prolongation of unjust actions. By heaping insult and ignominy upon the blacks, more fear is created and consequently more hatred.

"Only after we accept the Negro as a person and treat him as an equal and a brother in Christ can we hope to stamp out race hatred. Our hope then lies in the Church. . . ."

"But the Church has not accepted us!" Augustine protested impulsively.

"Wait a minute, Augustine; when you say the Church, you are saying Christ, for the Church is Christ. When you say that the Church has not accepted the Negroes, you really mean that some members in the Church have failed to do so. The Church always stands for right and justice. Members of the Church, however, since they are human beings, often fall short of the ideals of Christ in his Church."

The student raised his head and listened intently.

"The truth of the matter", continued Father Richardt, "is that members of the Church in America have made giant plans in behalf of the Negroes. An example is the Second Plenary Council of Baltimore held in 1866. However, when local bishops and priests tried to enforce the decrees of this council, they met with such fierce opposition and prejudice that little progress could be made. But in the intervening years, many members of the Church—religious and lay— have tried to better the lot of Negro people. Certain members of the Church, because they are human, will help or hinder the work of Christ in accordance with each one's own attitude toward his fellow men and his concern for his own spiritual welfare."

"Father," asked Augustine, "does this explain my own position? The reason why seminaries and religious orders refuse to admit me?"

"Yes, indeed," answered Father Richardt, "it does explain all of that. Bishops, priests, and monks are human beings. Some of them are most likely actuated by inborn prejudices against blacks, others by fear. Let me assure you, though, Augustine, that most of the members of the clergy are imbued with the spirit of Christ, and we heartily deplore the race situation. We are silently but staunchly fighting your cause—our cause."

Augustine smiled at last. He rose to leave because the class period had ended, but Father Richardt detained him. "Augustine," he began laying a hand on the young man's shoulder, "you and I are equally concerned about the injustices perpetrated by my race and the injustices heaped on your people. Let us face the situation like men—like Christians; let us do our part to spread the kingdom of God on earth. You have already made a magnificent start, Augustine. Look at Saint Joseph's School! That was your work. Look at all the good you are doing here in Quincy. That will live on and on."

Augustine gathered his books and turned to leave, but Father Richardt had a parting thought: "Many famous persons—churchmen and statesmen—are sincerely concerned about the race question. They are convinced that the solution of it depends upon a higher power—God. He sees man, not his color. As for statesmen, they must agree with the clear-seeing Thomas Jefferson, who ended one of his famous speeches in this way: 'In regard to the institution of slavery, indeed, I tremble for my country when I reflect that God is just.'"

"That God is just—that God is just." The words rang through Augustine's mind all the way home.

11

THROUGH THE DARKNESS
TO THE LIGHT

The year 1879 was a crucial one for Augustine Tolton. He was twenty-five years old. The regular tutoring by dedicated priests and nuns, his habitual self-discipline, his faithful observance of religious duties, and his twelve years of honest service as a wage earner had formed a character distinguished by determination, integrity, and leadership.

The rapid growth and success of Saint Joseph's School, which, as Father Richardt stated, owed its existence to his efforts, gave Augustine a sense of achievement. Helping victims free themselves from drink and lust rewarded him with the pure joy of service to others. His manly bearing and natural cheerfulness commanded love and respect from those around him, no matter what shade of color their skins might be.

Thus in the course of his apostolic activities, many of which seemed promising, Augustine began to experience an exuberant sense of usefulness and an awareness of his own independence. But by the same token he became more fully convinced of the fact that he was not receiving systematic and proper preparation for his life's work.

Two years earlier, on July 29, 1877, Augustine Tolton's basic drive had received a new impetus—a "jolt" as he described it later—whose effects increased with the passage of time. It occurred on the occasion of the first solemn Mass celebrated by his friend, Father Jerome Hellhake, a Franciscan, at Saint Boniface Church. The event had made an indelible impression and initiated, a new phase of spiritual restlessness and longing for the fulfillment of his dreams.

"What am I waiting for?" he asked himself again and again. "What are the Franciscans—Father Liborius and the others—planning for me? What does Father McGirr have in mind for me? They all know that I want to be a priest, but no one ever mentions it. Why don't they advise me and guide me? Bishop Baltes knows about me. Even Father Janssen, the vicar general, has told him that I am a candidate for the priesthood. But no one seems to be interested. Why are they so indifferent?"

A sudden violent upsurge of self-determination forced Augustine to take the initiative. He called on his pastor, Father McGirr. The priest was surprised at the young man's unusual self-assertiveness and insistence.

"Father," he began, "isn't it about time that I begin to study for the priesthood in a seminary? I think I have saved about enough money now to go to England, to the Saint Joseph's Society. How do I go about joining those fathers and getting into their seminary?"

Father McGirr, never one to equivocate, made the blunt reply: "I don't think the Josephite fathers have any idea or intention of recommending you for their society. It is all of five years since Father Wegmann made an application for you—at the suggestion of Bishop Baltes. You remember, don't you, Augustine, that from the beginning their superior, Father Noonan, advised you to study for the secular or diocesan priesthood. Of course they had no seminary in this country then and still don't have a training center for American candidates to the priesthood."

"Father," said Augustine anxiously, "I thought it was understood that I would be admitted to their foundation in England. I thought they would train me to be a missionary priest. In his letter to Father Wegmann, the superior in Baltimore asked if I was willing to go to Borneo, and Father answered him that I was ready to do that."

"Yes, and we have several direct communications with the superior of the Society in England," Father McGirr admitted, "and recently they have made it clear that in your case it would be far better if you continued to study right here in America. Those Josephites refer to this country as one of their missions because millions of freed slaves are in dire need of spiritual help. They seem to think that you belong here and that you will be better equipped for missionary work if you get your training in this country. That is why we are having you take classes at the Franciscan College now."

Augustine's face lighted up with new anticipation. "You mean, Father," he shouted, "that I can perhaps be admitted to the Franciscan seminary in Teutopolis?"

"No, I don't think you will", answered the priest slowly. "Father Schaeffermeyer recommended you long ago and many times since; Father Richardt and other priests who know you well have done the same. Nothing has come of it."

At that Augustine seemed to crumple, and Father McGirr knew that he would need all his powers of persuasion to restore the young man's confidence and to restore his hopes anew. He had hoped to acquaint Augustine with the true state of affairs and at the same time uphold the policies and practices of the religious leaders—even those with which he himself did not agree.

"The decision concerning admission of Negro members", began Father McGirr with manifest deliberation, "rests with the superiors of monasteries or maybe even with the provincial superior of the order. The Franciscans, for example, may do only what the provincial sanctions in such matters as concern the whole province. This same reason most likely accounts for the apparent indifference on the part of the Josephites. Many of the individual members of any order may welcome you sincerely, but everyone must abide by the decision of higher authority.

"Far be it from me to defend a religious order, but Augustine, you must understand their position. The Franciscan friary at Teutopolis is a comparatively new foundation here in America. The fathers and brothers have experienced hardships and difficulties since they arrived from Germany. The pioneer group was harassed not only by poverty, language barriers, and inconveniences of all kinds; at times they were suspected and grossly misunderstood. They certainly were not always received kindly by us diocesan priests, by the bishops, or by the people they came to serve. So you can see, Augustine, those early Franciscans had a rough start. They could scarcely earn enough to make a living, and for this they had to depend solely on missionary work."

The word "missionary" caused Augustine to straighten himself up and look intently at the speaker. Father McGirr, thinking he had aroused the youth's interest in the policies of the Franciscans, went on: "These priests were not accustomed to the American attitude toward blacks. They deplored the fearful race hatreds and antagonisms. White people threatened them with fines and even violence when, in some areas, they befriended Negro people. This, as well as the many legal restrictions which controlled racial relationships, obviously are among the reasons prompting their superiors to refuse to accept black applicants. This was the situation in the beginning, and I dare say that the period of

reconstruction in the South has intensified popular resentment against your race. The Franciscans—some of them—
seemed to think that their work in the cause of Christ would
be hindered, that their membership would decrease and their
influence diminish if blacks were seen in their ranks."

"Can anyone spread Christianity by being un-Christian?"
asked Augustine bitterly.

"You are right, Gus, you are absolutely right!" shouted
Father McGirr, who in his reaction to the youth's question
used his nickname for the first time. "They really couldn't
do Christ's work, that is, those members who were responsible for the un-Christian decisions. To support themselves
they often took the place of assistant pastors, or they became traveling missionaries, usually going great distances
on horseback. At times . . . Wait a minute, Gus!" called the
priest, detaining the youth, who out of sheer distress rose
to leave the rectory. Father McGirr did not want the young
man to leave without some reassurance.

"I want to tell you, Gus," he said, "that we are trying to
do something for you. Just last week I commissioned Father
Richardt to write to the bishop and ask him to plead your
cause at the Propaganda. This seminary is in Rome, and it
is the foremost missionary training center in the world. On
previous occasions Bishop Baltes made it clear that the diocese of Alton would pay for the seminary training of Negroes. It is possible that he will make an effort and perhaps
succeed in having you admitted to the pontifical college as
a candidate from this missionary country. The bishop is going to Rome for his five-year visit, and he promised Father
Richardt, in a letter he just received yesterday, that he would
call on the cardinal prefect of the Propaganda College. He
will try to have you enrolled and trained as a missionary
priest for the blacks of this country."

Until this moment Augustine had stood before Father McGirr with bowed head and slumped shoulders. When he heard the word "missionary priest", he looked up quickly and flashed a broad smile. He took one quick step toward the priest.

"Oh, Father, that's what I want. That's what I've been praying for. When will the bishop leave?" he asked breathlessly.

"Most likely next week", answered the priest. "Father Richardt said he got his letter to the chancery just in time. And the bishop answered immediately."

Day after day for the next several weeks Augustine lived in a state of alternate painful suspense and eager anticipation. "How long does it take to cross the ocean?" he asked himself again and again. "How long will the bishop stay in Rome? When will I find out? Will I really be accepted?"

During the long hours at the bottling works, Augustine continued to reason with himself. "Doesn't the whole world know how much priests are needed in Africa and every other country?" He remembered Father McGirr's telling him long ago—in fact, it was on the day of his first Communion —that there were black priests in Africa working side by side with white missionaries and that the black clergy were trained in Rome.

Augustine could not think of a single reason why he should be rejected. His hopes were raised still higher when he thought of those reports and letters of recommendation that Father Richardt had submitted to the bishop— references from his pastor, instructors, and friends among the clergy. He really had nothing to fear. In the exuberance of his spirits he shared the cherished secret with his mother. For hours sometimes far into the night, mother and son talked about it and waited and planned and prayed.

Disappointments continued, however, even in this suspense-laden period of his life. Because of the additional duties assigned to them at Saint Francis College, Father Engelbert Gey and Father Francis Albers were forced to terminate the private classes which they had conducted for Augustine Tolton for more than a year. Father Richardt, however, continued his sessions and not only gave the young student further instruction in the fields of theology and philosophy but also directed him in his apostolic work in Quincy. Above all, he counseled him in his spiritual development. Father Richardt looked upon the youth as a friend, a zealous coworker, a brother in Christ, and a future priestly companion.

Then, late in 1879, came the news of Father Janssen's transfer from Saint Boniface parish and the appointment of Father Theodore Bruener as his successor. Both Father Richardt and Augustine wondered how Saint Joseph School would fare without the deep interest and generous help of Father Janssen. Augustine was even more concerned because on more than one occasion Father Richardt intimated that the provincial superior planned to withdraw the Franciscan priests from Saint Joseph's School.

"Oh, Father, I hope that does not happen", said Augustine incredulously. "We just have a good start now."

"Well, it all depends upon the next pastor", said Father Richardt. "Saint Boniface parish maintained the place all this while. We Franciscans merely contributed our services."

Saint Joseph's School had suffered more setbacks than either Father Richardt or Augustine wanted to admit. Ever since its opening, those people who were unfriendly toward Catholicism looked with disfavor on the project. During the final months of 1879, non-Catholics had been particularly effective in their efforts to lure children of any age away from the school. As they invited the Catholic pupils to their own Sunday School classes and to their young people's organizations, the number of first communicants in Saint Joseph's School decreased even though the total enrollment remained stationary. Places left vacant by children who were coaxed away soon filled up because of Augustine's intensified recruiting.

Father Richardt and his student deplored the unsound condition of the project they had initiated. Yet, they both continued to work with unabated zeal. "Any good work that we can still do is not lost and must not be left undone", said the priest. It was a motive apparently energizing both teacher and lay apostle.

Augustine still reported regularly for his lessons. At one session, as he waited in the priest's study with his load of books, Father Richardt came wearily into the room and dropped into the chair behind his desk. He had brought no books, and his response to Augustine's greeting was almost inaudible. For some time he fumbled in his pockets and finally produced a letter—a letter that had obviously been folded and unfolded many times.

"Augustine, I have this letter from Bishop Baltes", he said softly.

The student rose to his feet and took a step forward.

"It seems he tried very hard to get you admitted to the Propaganda College," the priest continued, "but he did not succeed yet. He was told that you ought to be trained in America; the millions of freed slaves need priests. The bishop writes that you should wait. In a few years the Josephites in Baltimore will most likely open a seminary."

Augustine, who had been standing motionless, fell back a little and covered his face with his hands. He tried to speak;

the words stuck in his throat. He bumped against the table, and his pile of books fell to the floor with a resounding crash. He made no attempt to retrieve them. "Father Richardt," he said in a hoarse whisper, "I think I'd better go home."

Before Father Richardt could detain him, Augustine was out of the room and out on the street. His anguish was expressed in his slow, even dragging steps. At home he sat on the edge of a chair; his head hung low, his arms folded across his chest. He did not need to tell his mother that he had received the devastating news. For a long time he sat in deep silent thought; his mother looked on in helpless agony. "The goodness of the Lord", she said softly. "It endures forever."

Father Richardt was deeply affected by the grief that the bishop's letter had brought to Augustine Tolton. The pain and anguish in the young man's face haunted him and drove him into action. He decided to carry out his plan immediately—a plan which he held in reserve and one by which he believed Augustine could still be admitted to the Propaganda College.

What he had resolved to do if all else failed was appeal directly to the superior of the whole Franciscan Order, Bernadino dal Vago da Porto Romantino, at their headquarters in Rome. "Augustine can go to the pontifical seminary", Father Richardt thought to himself, "if Father Bernardin tells the cardinal prefect that the candidate is Negro and that he is eager to go to Africa as a missionary priest."

As soon as Father Richardt reached his room in Saint Francis Friary, he closed the door upon himself and began the letter—a task that was to stretch far into the night. The bulky message contained a complete account of Augustine Tolton—his life history, character, reputation, education, and qualifications. Father Richardt referred to him as a reverent acolyte, a devoted son, a faithful worker, a diligent student, and a zealous lay apostle. The report included a full description of what had already been done toward getting the black candidate admitted to a seminary; he told about the efforts of the bishop with the subsequent results—the accurate reasons for the rejection. Then he appended a list of names for references and finally expressed his own sincere desire and prayerful wish that Augustine Tolton be admitted to the Propaganda College.

For more than two months after his latest rejection, Augustine suffered gnawing grief and complete disillusionment. Several times he was on the verge of despair. Day after day he came to and from the factory, the church, or his class in a mechanical way and to all appearances in a state of shock. Persons with whom he came into contact noticed his quick, feverish activity; strained features; and forced smile. He was tense and nervous. His thin frame showed loss of appetite, lack of sleep, and inner conflict.

"The unmistakable will of God", he moaned in times of extreme desolation. "How can this divine will be opposed and hindered by the will of men—churchmen?"

In later years Augustine referred to this period of his life as a season of annealing. It was a year during which his faith was repeatedly subjected to the severest test, a year during which days and weeks of disillusionment and frustration at times drove him to the brink of madness. But it was also an opportunity for gaining moral strength and courage to help him battle the still more difficult years that lay ahead.

Father Richardt knew only too well that Augustine was enduring bitter trial and turmoil, and so he overlooked the fact that lessons were neglected, that interest and inspiration had waned. During the instruction periods the priest spoke to the troubled man with paternal kindness and understanding; he tried to lift the weight of sorrow and despair by recalling all the good work Augustine had done and was able to do for those of his race.

One evening when Augustine seemed more depressed than ever, when his whole being was engulfed in impenetrable darkness, Father Richardt decided that he would have to do something now.

"Augustine, I have something to tell you", he said gently. "I am waiting for a letter from the superior general of the Franciscan Order in Rome. I happened to know that he is acquainted with the prefect of the Propaganda College. I wrote to him some time ago asking him to plead your cause. After all, I'm a Franciscan too!"

This information brought the first smile Father Richardt had seen for many weeks.

As the days passed by, Augustine's spirits revived. He recalled and, with steadfast faith, clung to the statement Father Schaeffermeyer had made many years earlier: "If God vonts you to be a priest, you vill be von."

Then came that never-to-be-forgotten morning when Mrs. Tolton saw her son rushing up the street toward their shack. It was an unusual hour—a time when ordinarily he would have been at work. "Why is he running like that, skipping and capering like a child?" thought Mrs. Tolton as she hurried out to meet him.

"Mother!" he shouted. "I'm going to Rome! I'm going to be a priest!"

Mrs. Tolton looked at her son as though she had never seen him before. After a long moment, her eyes brimming with grateful tears, she half-whispered, "Augustine, never forget the goodness of the Lord."

12

OFF TO ROME

It was Sunday afternoon, February 15, 1880.

In the midst of a group of people who had gathered at the Fourth and Main Street railroad station stood Augustine Tolton, ready to leave for his journey to the Eternal City. He smiled bravely as he received the good wishes and last-minute farewells of his family and his friends—old and young, black and white, priests, college students, schoolchildren. A momentary hushed silence fell upon them as a child's high-pitched voice rang out, "I hear it a-coming."

There was a shrill whistle as the C. B. & Q. passenger train thundered into the city of Quincy, Illinois, and slowly came to a stop. Augustine made hurried farewells and then, with Father Michael Richardt at his side, walked rapidly toward the train. The parting sentiments of the two men transcended words; their mutual admiration was expressed in a viselike handclasp.

Just before entering the coach indicated by the conductor, Augustine looked back; his eyes searched for his mother, who, like her son, thought of this farewell as the last earthly leavetaking of an Africa-bound missionary. There she stood, immobile, in front of the crowd. Her dark face, a study in maternal pride and hard-earned victory, was furrowed with the pain of parting. Augustine remembered this image of his mother for the rest of his life.

The whole group moved quickly toward the train just to get a glimpse of Augustine inside the coach. They could see him in the dingy window nodding and smiling. The puffs of the locomotive and the warning whistle brought louder cheers and more enthusiastic waving. Through the billowing smoke and steam, Augustine saw the hand of Father McGirr raised in benediction. As the train began to move he could still hear the shouts of "Goodbye, Augustine!" and "Goodbye, Mr. Tolton!" and "Goodbye, Gus!" but the piping voices of children were quickly lost in the noisy clatter.

Passengers peering from every window of the coach showed surprise and astonishment at the scene they witnessed. Augustine's friends noticed that every person in the coach to which he had been directed was black. It was a Jim Crow car.

All the familiar sights and sounds of Augustine's childhood and youth vanished as the train picked up speed and dashed into the open countryside. Augustine, who had never been anywhere since the family's flight from slavery, was fascinated by the swiftly moving landscape and changing scenery. He studied the timetable and marked the larger towns through which he would pass in the 230 miles to Chicago—Burlington (on the Iowa side of the Mississippi), then Galesburg, Mendota, and Aurora in Illinois.

During the journey Augustine wandered up and down the aisle of the coach to talk with fellow passengers. Most of them were unkempt, indifferent, drowsy—and frightened. They had come from the South to find jobs in Chicago. Their dull, glazed eyes showed the apathy of the unskilled, the unlettered, and the unhappy. The words "Rome", and "priesthood", and "missionary" did not have the faintest meaning for them. Augustine's heart was filled with compassion. How he wished he could share the overflowing joy of his whole being with these—his less fortunate brothers.

Alone in his seat, when the excitement of the day had subsided, Augustine relaxed and organized his thoughts. He relived every incident of the two months that had passed since
the day he received the news of his acceptance in the Propaganda College in Rome. He smiled to himself as he recalled that morning at the Flynn bottling works, when Father
Richardt came swiftly toward him in the basement area: the
way he waved that letter before his eyes as he was washing
bottles and all but shouted the news: "Here it is, Gus, here
it is! You're going! You're going to Rome!"

It was sheer joy just to think of that day: how he wanted to
grab the letter even with his hands dripping; how he jerked
off his water-drenched apron and threw it somewhere before joining Father Richardt; how they read the letter together again and again. Then how the manager came along
to release him from work for the rest of the day; how he
had rushed home to tell his mother and how he had run
over to tell Father McGirr. And how happy Father McGirr
was; how he clapped his hands in glee and unconsciously
performed a little Irish jig.

A wave of gratitude flooded Augustine's heart as he recalled the help and encouragement he received once the
news of his acceptance in the Propaganda College was announced. Father Janssen, still vicar general of the diocese,
informed Bishop Baltes; and sometime later came the letters of recommendation the bishop had signed with instruction that Augustine present these to the cardinal prefect of
Propaganda College. Then Bishop Baltes had donated fifty
dollars in diocesan funds to defray his traveling expenses.
Students of Saint Francis College took up a collection for additional funds. Father Mueller, the rector, added the "Franciscan mite" of ten dollars to the sum. These contributions,

together with his own earnings over the years, were more than enough to pay for the voyage, provide a seminarian's wardrobe, and take care of other expenses.

As the train jogged on through the cities and towns, Augustine recalled other friends and benefactors. He searched in his pockets for the letters he had received before he left Quincy—letters he must not lose, letters he would always treasure. He began to read them again: "I will make a memento in my Mass for you every day", wrote Father Liborius Schaeffermeyer from Teutopolis. "I congratulate you on your good fortune, and I am convinced that you will do well. I want to hear from you when you are in Rome."

Augustine was affected anew by the letter from Father Francis Ostrop, former pastor of Saint Boniface parish and now stationed at Carlinville, Illinois. "I promised Father Schaeffermeyer some years ago that I would look after you, and I mean to keep my word. You will hear from me now and then while you are in the seminary, and I will supply you with pocket money. The enclosed is a starter." The priest sent Augustine a fifty-dollar check.

The next letter that Augustine selected from the packet was from Sister Perpetua of Saint Mary's Hospital, Hoboken, New Jersey. He read the message again and again!

Dear Augustine:

It made me very happy to hear that you will go to Rome and study for the priesthood. Sister Eusebia wrote to tell me that you will be in Hoboken for a few days before you set sail. We want you to be our guest here at the hospital for those days. I am looking forward with much pleasure to the time when I will meet you again. It is all of four years since I last saw you. How well I remember the many times you came to our hospital in Quincy while you were taking instruction from Father Reinhart. May God protect you on your journey both on land and on the ocean.

Yours respectfully,
Sister Perpetua, O.S.F.

It was night when the train chugged into the Chicago station. Here Augustine had a two-hour wait. He grabbed his traveling case and hurried out with the others. The sights and sounds all around threw him into a state of awe and utter confusion. First he inquired about his next train and then joined a group of blacks at a lunch counter. After that he jostled his way through the throngs of travelers and finally boarded the New York Central train. An eight-hundred-mile ride would bring him to Jersey City and the port of Hoboken.

On Tuesday morning, February 17, Augustine alighted from the carriage that had stopped in front of Saint Mary's Hospital at Fourth and Willow Streets in Hoboken. Before he had a chance to sound the knocker, the door opened swiftly, and Sister Perpetua, wreathed in smiles, stood before him, saying, "Gott sei Dank, Augustine, komm herein."

For the next four days Augustine was the guest of Sister Perpetua and the other Franciscan sisters who staffed the hospital. All these German-born women were delighted when they discovered that Augustine spoke German. In fact, German was the only language they used while Augustine was their guest. Each morning the Rome-bound student served Mass in the hospital chapel, and during the day he visited some of the churches of the city. In all, he thoroughly enjoyed the Franciscan hospitality, which he later described as "fit for a bishop". And then, as Sister Perpetua bade her guest farewell, she promised, "I will pray for you, every day, Augustine, so that you'll persevere in your vocation and that you'll become a good priest."

Augustine responded in a tone of matching sincerity: "Sister, if I become a priest, and if I should ever happen to return to the United States, I will celebrate Holy Mass here in your chapel."

The ship *Der Westlicher*, scheduled to depart for Le Havre on Saturday, February 21, lay at anchor in the port at Hoboken. Augustine joined the other Europe-bound travelers and observed their actions so as not to be rattled by the custom house regulations and procedures. Several hours passed before the passengers walked across the gangplank into the huge vessel. Augustine's expression and his whole bearing betrayed inexperience and anxiety. The blowing of the whistle proclaimed that all travelers were on board; the clang of the engine's pistons and wheels, the churning of propellers, and the forward glide of the ship convinced everyone that the three-thousand-mile crossing had begun.

When Augustine noticed different nationalities and races among the passengers, he relaxed and began to feel more secure. The natural fright occasioned by the rocking of the vessel in the vast ocean subsided as he observed the unconcern of the more seasoned travelers. And then, just as he was maneuvering his way through the crowd to locate his cabin, Augustine was startled to hear a man's voice calling, "Augustine! Here, this way, Augustine!" Not far away he saw three Franciscan priests. As they came nearer he immediately recognized Father Ewald Fahle, whom he had met in Quincy; the other two were strangers to him, but they did not remain so very long. All three priests, exiles of the 1875 *Kulturkampf*, were on their way back to Germany for a visit with relatives.

During the course of the voyage other passengers were puzzled by this very "different" group—three brown-robed and barefoot "Nordic" friars and a very black layman. What

was more, they spoke German with each other and frater-
nized, prayed, and sang together at regular times each day.
People stood around on the deck of the ship and listened as
the four men joined their voices in harmony singing hymns
and at times secular songs.

The twelve-day voyage ended at Le Havre on March 4.
At this port the three priests assisted Augustine in finding a
place to stay for the night and with a heartfelt "Auf Wieder-
sehen" parted company with him. In order to make railway
connections to Rome, Augustine had a layover of a day and
a night in the French capital of Paris.

The vibrant city, with its large crowds and noisy activity,
all but overwhelmed the inexperienced American. During
the short strolls he took in the neighborhood of his hotel
and the railroad station, some people eyed him with curiosity; others took no notice of him whatsoever. They may
have thought that he belonged to a crew of workmen; or,
because he was well dressed, they may have regarded him
as a member of a circus troupe.

Then the last lap of the long journey from Quincy, Illinois, ended on March 10, when the train stopped in Rome
at 9:00 P.M. A policeman helped Augustine find a carriage
to take him to the seminary. But first he entered one of
Rome's famous churches. Augustine Tolton's heart was so
filled with joy and thanksgiving that he did not even learn
the name of the church, nor did he then notice the location,
the flamboyant architecture, or its high Baroque altar. He
simply fell on his knees. "My Lord, Jesus Christ," he said,
"I got here."

13

THE SEMINARIAN

"Verso dove, Signore?" shouted the coachman, looking noncommittally at the tall black man standing before the door of a Roman hotel.

"To the Piazza di Spagna", answered Augustine promptly, guessing the meaning of the driver's question. He referred to his notebook and added, "To the Collegium Urbanum de Propaganda Fide."

The Piazza di Spagna, near the Collegium Urbanum

Collegium Urbanum de Propaganda Fide

The coachman nodded saying, "Sì, sì, Signore", as he jerked the reins and uttered sounds understood only by the horses.

As the conveyance clattered over the uneven streets, Augustine gazed in awe and astonishment at the conglomeration of buildings around him. When the driver pointed out Saint Peter's dome silhouetted in the distance, the young man drew a quick breath and was unable to say anything but "Oh . . . ! Oh . . . !"

The carriage stopped at the foot of the so-called Spanish steps. While the obliging driver waited, Augustine admired the historic church of *Trinita dei Monte* that overlooks the *Piazza di Spagna*. Then the coachman pointed out another building, and soon the carriage moved toward it. "There it is!" cried Augustine excitedly as the driver stopped at the entrance to a three-story structure. Augustine had noticed the large plaque high above the front door. It bore the Roman-lettered inscription: COLLEGIUM URBANUM DE PROPAGANDA FIDE.

A smiling seminarian met the new student at the door and showed him into a small waiting room. Augustine shifted his traveling case from one hand to the other; finally he set it on the floor. He went to the chair indicated by the seminarian, sat nervously on the edge, and waited. Above the pounding of his heart he heard the rustling of brocaded robes. In another moment Cardinal Giovanni Simeoni, prefect of the college, entered. As Augustine jumped to his feet, the great prelate came forward, clasped a black hand in both his own, and welcomed the American candidate to the Propaganda College.

It was Friday, March 12, and as was pointed out by Father John Greene, S.S.J., editor of the Josephite publication *The Saint Joseph Advocate*,[1]

> The day is significant; the 12th being the feast of Pope Gregory the Great, one of the most determined enemies of slavery who ever sat in the Chair of Peter. It was he who uttered the famous sentence on seeing the English slaves for sale: "*Non Angli sed Angeli si Christiani forent.* No Angles (Anglo-Saxons) but angels would they be if only they were Christians." And it was Saint Gregory who set the example of manumission by giving freedom to all slaves attached to his patrimony.

It was on this date, then, that Augustine Tolton, ex-slave, began his preparation for the priesthood.

[1] April, 1887.

In the course of the first few days Augustine was introduced to many people associated with the college. He had no
idea of their status, despite the fact that they were garbed in
black or red or purple. Even though he had previously studied and rehearsed the proper procedures for meeting and ad-
dressing members of the hierarchy, the flustered young man
forgot the terminology completely and responded with a
stammering "Yes, Father" or "No, Father" to seminarians,
priests, monsignors, archbishops, and cardinals alike.

On Palm Sunday, March 21, that year, just nine days after
his arrival in Rome, Augustine Tolton was invested with the
uniform of the Collegium Urbanum de Propaganda Fide—
a black soutane with red sash and a black biretta with red
tassel. Every student wore this uniform as a mark of distinction both in private and in public, during the whole period
of seminary training. No earthly potentate could have worn
his costly robes with greater pride than that which Augustine experienced when he donned the uniform of the papal
seminary.

As the days passed, Augustine gradually became acquainted
with his companions, his teachers, and his surroundings.
He felt more at home in the lecture halls, library, chapel,
museum, and recreation areas. The initial anxiety, which
tended to paralyze his mind and speech, subsided. In a flood
of relief and new happiness, he discovered that the seventy or
more seminarians in attendance at the pontifical college represented many races and nationalities, all of whom accepted
him unconditionally and sincerely. The profound bow or
the slight nod, the handshake or friendly smile proved the
good will of students from Africa, Europe, Asia, and the
Americas. The discrimination and prejudice that he had so
often suffered in the United States during all the years of
his childhood and youth were unknown in the Propaganda
College.

For the first time in his life Augustine sensed the sublime delight of the brotherhood of man under the fatherhood of God. He prayed and worked, played and sang, ate and slept in a society—a society with a common bond and a common goal. He experienced the security of equality and justice, a sense of dignity and worth, the comfort and companionship of friends, the joy of mutual charity and benevolence. He profited by the ready helpfulness of classmates with whom he could study and discuss, give, accept, and share. The oppressive weight of segregation was removed; the race barriers were gone. He never felt lonely, unwanted, or out of place. He was treated as a person, as a member of the Church, as a child of God. Augustine Tolton admitted then, and frequently in later years, that during all his seminary days he had received a full measure of earthly happiness.

As time passed, Augustine learned more and more about the history and purpose of the papal seminary. He found out why it was at times called Urban College and why it was given a place within the Congregatio de Propaganda Fide. He learned that this department of papal administration was established in the seventeenth century and that it is charged with the propagation of Catholicism and the regulation of spiritual affairs in non-Catholic countries.

Augustine was deeply interested in books dealing with the subject of missionary work. His pencil raced back and forth in his notebook as he studied in the library. "More than two billion inhabitants of the world are subject to the Sacred Congregation of the Propagation of the Faith," he wrote, "and besides many districts and sections of certain countries, it has jurisdiction over nearly all of Africa, Australia, New Zealand, Oceania, Japan, China, India, and Indochina." The student read the whole passage again. Then he encircled the word "Africa".

"The United States of America," the text went on, "where

the hierarchy was established in 1789, is still defined as 'missionary territory' because the Church there is still in her formative years." Augustine winced at the thought of the Church in America.

Then one day he read about Pope Urban VIII. The College of the Sacred Congregation *de Propaganda Fide* is called the Urban College because it was founded by Pope Urban. Augustine learned that the main purpose of this college is to bring candidates for the priesthood from mission countries to live and study in Rome—the center of Christendom. The student understood very well that candidates for the priesthood studying in the Urban College get an idea of the greatness of the Church, which is something they could not appreciate if they saw it only in the humble missionary activities in their homelands. Augustine copied this bit of information in his notebook and then with a swift stroke of his pencil underscored every word of the whole paragraph.

The more Augustine read about the Propaganda College, the more he appreciated his own association with it. Yet there was one nagging question—a question for which no one had an answer: "Am I here as a candidate for the diocesan priesthood in missionary America because Bishop Baltes of the Alton diocese paid one-fourth of my passage? Or am I here because the Franciscans recommended me as a missionary priest for Africa?"

Augustine was not unduly perturbed by the question. And it seemed more and more obvious that he was indeed Africa-bound. The courses he was assigned to pursue, the seminarians with whom he was grouped, the languages and dialects he was encouraged to learn, all pointed to the fact that he was destined to be an African missionary.

Every other student and every professor at the Urban College knew before very long that Augustine was proud of his

Augustine Tolton as a seminarian

race, proud that God had given his people so much room on this globe and proud that he could work as an *alter Christus* in that vast territory. The consciousness of his place and work in the papal college and later in the Lord's vineyard inspired him to ever greater diligence and dedication.

Back in Quincy, Illinois, every letter from Augustine received by his mother or his pastor or the Franciscan fathers brought gladness and jubilation. His loved ones treasured and shared the glowing accounts that every message brought. Augustine referred to his Italian teachers as "loving" and "fatherly". The professors whom he frequently named and quoted were Father Conrado, Father Levi, and Monsignor Satolli. In one letter he mentioned the "very kind Professor Bourghi" and also his teacher in moral theology, Father Checchi. He described Father Checchi as "very learned and also very considerate" and often referred to him as "my best friend". Augustine also wrote about his fellow students as "exceedingly fine men—kind and helpful". In later years, Augustine, commenting on his seminary days, stated, "All were my friends; they loved me, though I cannot say why."

From the very outset, professors and students alike called the American seminarian "Gus" or "Gus from the U.S."— nicknames that persisted through all the years of Augustine's stay in Rome.

On May 6, 1883, when he was a third-year seminarian, Augustine was permitted to take the so-called Propaganda Oath. As members of the pontifical household, all students of the Urban College bind themselves to these promises: (1) they shall work in whatever country or diocese is assigned to them by the Sacred Congregation; (2) once they return to their respective countries they will not enter any religious community without the permission of the Holy See or of the Sacred Congregation; (3) they shall inform the Sacred Congregation at least every three years, if they are missioned outside of Europe, of their general condition and work in their respective dioceses.

Augustine took the solemn pledge with a carefree spirit. In fact, he regarded it as significant and a long step toward his goal—missionary work in Africa.

After that, Augustine intensified his reading on the "Dark Continent", and he mingled even more with seminarians from Africa in order to acquaint himself with the culture, language, and dialects of that country. He seemed intent upon getting through the whole 30,000 books in the seminary library, and he lingered over the assortment of artifacts sent home by missionary priests from various countries. It was obvious that he studied the history and geography of Africa with a special zest and determination, and so it was a generally accepted fact that Augustine's future was in Africa, not in America.

From the outset Augustine adjusted easily to the daily routine of seminary life. As he was always an early riser, the first bell was heeded as readily and cheerfully as those marking the times for prayer, Mass, meditation, spiritual reading, meals, and recreation. Augustine converted every action and every task of the day, easy or difficult, into a stepping stone leading him forward to his goal.

One accomplishment which impressed the seminarians and which afforded him and his friends many hours of pleasure was his skill as an accordion player. Over a period of months and years, Augustine had mastered the instrument with the help of a fellow student. He learned to play not only the music of his own country; his repertoire included the songs of many other nations represented at the Urban College. During hours of recreation Augustine and his accordion were always in demand. Students and teachers listened with pleasure as Augustine's nimble fingers ran over the keys in accompaniment to his own beautiful singing of Negro spirituals.

Though the American student was not set apart as a prodigy of learning or scholarship, he was nevertheless distinguished for his exemplary life. Everyone admired his daily little acts of goodness that showed his worth and the larger virtues that revealed his character. Augustine's spiritual life was deepened and his knowledge of religion was enriched in various ways: with groups of other seminarians and priests he visited many of the six hundred or more churches in Rome. He was always to treasure the notebook in which he made sketches of Rome's ecclesiastical art and architecture or recorded brief histories of the sacred places he visited and studied. His trips to the catacombs made a lasting impression; he wrote detailed accounts of the burial places in the underground passages and made diagrams of the altars and shrines marking the tombs of the early Christian martyrs. For Augustine, this was the real significance of the city.

Diligent study and daily discipline molded Augustine into a man of stability, a man of moral strength and courage. Consequently, he was accounted worthy of being received into the ranks of the clergy. On May 14, 1883, Augustine was among the seminarians who received the tonsure—a symbol that he had been raised from the lay to the clerical state. At the end of the simple ceremony, Cardinal Lenti addressed the new clerics, now vested in cassock and surplice. Augustine never forgot these words of the prelate's closing prayer: "Let us pray to our Lord Jesus Christ, that he may send them the Holy Spirit, to free their hearts from the bonds of the world and from earthly desires."

14

SAINT JOSEPH'S SCHOOL IN QUINCY

"This is for you, Augustine," said Cardinal Simeoni, prefect of the Urban College, as he handed the seminarian a letter with a Quincy, Illinois, postmark.

It was September, 1880, Augustine's first year in Rome. The American student had not yet fully conquered the occasional spells of homesickness that plagued him whenever he thought of the thousands of miles separating him from his family and friends.

"It's from Father Michael", exclaimed Augustine with manifest pleasure, as he took the letter, tore the envelope open, and began to read. After the first page his smile faded, and a look of deep disappointment settled on his face.

"They had to close Saint Joseph's School", he told his friends, all of whom were well acquainted with the project. "The provincial superior, Father Vincent Halbfas, has ordered the Franciscan fathers to discontinue their association with the school. Sister Herlinde has left Quincy, and the building stands there vacant again."

Augustine folded the letter and walked away. He reflected ruefully upon the time and effort expended during the three years of the school's existence. "Father Michael worked too hard", he said, walking toward a group of English-speaking students who had watched him in mute sympathy. "He mentions 'overwork and nervousness', and he also says he is being transferred from Quincy to Teutopolis, where he will teach in the Franciscan seminary. I know Sister Herlinde is very disappointed. The last thing she said to me when I left was, 'Pray for us, Augustine, that we can keep the school open.' As soon as I find out where Sister Herlinde is teaching, I will write her a letter," he said loyally, "because I know she is very sad."

For a long time Augustine heard no more about Saint Joseph's School. His companions, who had shared his early enthusiasm as well as his later disappointments, tactfully avoided the subject out of consideration for his feelings.

Augustine became more and more engrossed in his work. Prayer, meditations, and study, excursions in the Eternal City, and the routine of seminary life completely occupied the young cleric. He was wholly unaware of the fact that in Quincy, carpenters and painters were at work; that dedicated priests and generous people were planning a church and school for black people.

No one on either side of the Atlantic had the slightest idea that the remodeling of a small church in Quincy had major significance for a student in Rome—a seminarian preparing for missionary work in Africa.

Then one day in 1883, Augustine Tolton, a third-year student, received a letter from Father McGirr which brought the heartening news that not only had the day school been reopened, but an actual parish—church and school—for blacks had been established in Quincy. "The same old Protestant church building," wrote his old pastor, "which belongs to Saint Boniface parish, is completely remodeled and renovated."

Father Theodore Bruener, pastor of Saint Boniface parish, and credited with leadership in the Negro project in Quincy, gives a detailed account in his book *Kirchengeschichte Quincy's* of the developments there from the year 1880 to 1886.

Saint Joseph's one-room school closed in the fall of 1880. The Franciscan Fathers who taught religion found the additional burden too great, especially because of the school's distance from the friary. Accordingly, the provincial superior ordered them to withdraw.

Father Bruener was deeply concerned. Saint Boniface parish had maintained the school, and he appreciated the good work that had been done there. Consequently he conferred with two other priests, Father Cornelius Hoffmann, his assistant, and Father Joseph Still, pastor of Saint John's parish. All three priests deplored the closing of the school, but they believed that if anything permanent was to be effected, the black people must have a church as well as a school of their own. They also thought that there should be a resident pastor to conduct regular and complete Sunday service and, of course, teachers for the school.

During their meetings the priests decided to reconstruct the old building, renovate it as a church, and use the basement as a school. Saint Boniface parish would support it, and all three priests would take turns at conducting Sunday service. The plan received the consent and approbation of Peter J. Baltes, bishop of Alton.

The whole building had to be remodeled and redecorated; expensive repairs had to be made, such as new floors, new walls, new roof, and tower; and a cross had to be put on the spire. Both church and school had to be equipped. Where were the necessary funds to come from? Father Bruener's financial report shows that the people were interested in the project and that they made contributions toward it: "In the matter of money it must be mentioned that Mrs. Herman Tenk succeeded in collecting most of the funds. She has been aptly called 'Mother of Negroes' because of her concern for them. Furthermore the sisters of the school cleared $220.00 by conducting two entertainments in the parish hall. The bishop sent a check of $112.50. Several religious leaders of the diocese gave $10.00; Mr. Herman Hein and Mr. J.J. Stickner gave the pews; Mr. Kaspar Maas gave the cross and Mrs. J.K. Morrsmann, a widow, donated the monstrance."

Then, on January 15, 1882, Saint Joseph's Church was opened with a solemn High Mass and sermon. The building could not be dedicated as a church because of its insecure and faulty foundation. But from that day on, regular Sunday services—two Masses with sermons, afternoon vespers with Benediction, and a period of religious instruction —were conducted.

From the outset, Father Hoffmann devoted himself wholeheartedly to the new school. It was he who invited Sister Herlinde to return. With the permission of her superior, she came back and took charge of the children from whom she had tearfully parted two years earlier. Father Hoffmann taught in the school every day—catechism on three days of the week and Bible history on the other two days. Soon the school became too crowded for one sister. A candidate for the order of Notre Dame was engaged to teach the smaller children in a second classroom, which was constructed in the basement.

Father Bruener quickly discovered that he had taken on too heavy a responsibility. He encountered more than one problem: first, he himself could scarcely manage the additional work that the new parish entailed; then, Father Still, who was often called away when it was his turn to officiate, could not always find a substitute; finally, Father Hoffmann, generally in poor health, could not endure the many duties he had taken on. In the summer of 1883 he was compelled to give up completely. On the advice of a physician he made an ocean voyage in the fall and spent the winter in Germany. Father Francis Budde, assigned to take the sick priest's place, also found the work too heavy. When Father Hoffmann returned he was still not able to resume a full load even in his own parish.

In his predicament Father Bruener appealed to Bishop Baltes for a pastor to take charge of Saint Joseph's parish. The bishop replied that he could not do this simply because he did not have a priest available. Finally Father Bruener went to Saint Francis Friary in Quincy. Father Andrew Butzkueben, guardian, agreed to having Father Samuel Macke assist at Saint Joseph's Church every third Sunday under the condition that he be given the usual stipend.

Even in far-away Rome Augustine Tolton heard about Saint Joseph's Church and School in Quincy. He was overjoyed when, from the letter of Father McGirr, he learned about the project. News of further developments reached him later from various sources. He was particularly pleased with the letter from Father Michael Richardt of Teutopolis, which confirmed earlier reports and contained the surprising addition, "We Franciscans are working at Saint Joseph's Church. Father Samuel Macke helps out there." Augustine shared all the good news with his friends. Seminarians and professors alike rejoiced with him and continued to be interested in every detail of the new developments.

The sequel to this development is given in the final part of Father Bruener's report:

With the help of Father Samuel Macke Saint Joseph's parish experienced a period of progress. The burdens of the other priests associated with it were lightened considerably. Now they were able to resume more work in their own parishes and at a less hectic pace. Father Macke took over the Sunday Masses and sermons and taught religion in the school.

But all this lasted only one and a half years—from October 1884 until April 1885. The black parish was destined to suffer another setback. Father Bruener was told that Father

Macke would be transferred from Quincy and that it was not possible to provide a substitute. Therefore it became necessary to limit or shorten the services at Saint Joseph's Church. Sunday Masses and sermons were discontinued. A vesper service and Benediction followed by a period of religious instruction were conducted on Sunday afternoon. The blacks, however, did have a chance to fulfill their obligations, because they were not barred from other churches in Quincy. Sister Herlinde and her assistant kept the school open until the end of the term and reopened it again in fall.

Then in September 1885, when Father George Pesch was appointed assistant pastor at Saint Boniface parish, regular and complete Sunday services were held again. Besides that, evening instructions followed by Benediction were conducted twice a month in addition to the Sunday afternoon program. This attracted non-Catholic blacks as well as those who were regular church members. This schedule was followed until July 1886, when the first pastor was officially appointed to take charge of Saint Joseph's Church.

15

YOU ARE A PRIEST FOREVER

"Let those come forward who are to be ordained to the order of porter." Augustine Tolton responded "*Adsum*" when his name was announced after this canonical call. The three-day spiritual retreat, preparing candidates for the first two minor orders, had ended on that morning, March 8, 1884.

"Act so as to be able to account to God for what is guarded by these keys", exhorted Cardinal Lucido Parocchi as he handed the symbols—keys of the church—to each one of the seminarians assembled in the chapel of the Urban College.

With a lighted candle in his right hand, Augustine, knowing that he stood on the very threshold of the priesthood, listened with fervent attention as Cardinal Parocchi named the duties that would be his as porter: "Ring the bells, open and close the doors to the church and the sacristy, open the books for the preacher."

Augustine touched the keys and heard the cardinal's prayer: "Let us beseech God to bless this servant whom he has deigned to elect to the office of porter." Now he realized that he had indeed taken the first of seven steps leading to the priesthood; he understood that the duties and privileges of this order served as preliminary training for his final goal, and it spurred him on toward deeper spirituality. "Just as with material keys you open and close the visible house of

God," counseled the cardinal, "so endeavor by word and example to close to the devil and open to God the invisible dwelling of the Lord—namely, the hearts of the faithful."

In the second step of that day's ceremony Augustine again answered "*Adsum*", this time in response to the call for the order of lector. He listened intently as the cardinal listed the duties of the second minor order: "To read the word of God, that is, the sacred lessons, distinctly and intelligibly, so that the faithful may understand and be edified." Augustine laid a hand, trembling with the emotion of the moment, on the Sacred Scriptures while Cardinal Parocchi said, "Take and proclaim the word of God." Augustine must have been deeply impressed and even inspired by the final exhortation of the rite: "What you have read with your lips, you must believe in your hearts and practice in your works." Even though he may not have fully comprehended the symbolism, the prayers and exhortations of that day's ceremony, he was, nevertheless, more fully aware of the Church's wisdom in her calculated slowness—the step-by-step training of men for the priesthood.

Nine months later, on December 20, 1884, Augustine's "*Adsum*" followed the cardinal's call to the third minor order: "Let those come forward who are to be ordained to the order of exorcist." While the candidate held the symbol— the sacred book of rites—Cardinal Parocchi said, "You receive power to lay hands on those possessed. Through your imposition of hands the unclean spirits will, by the power of the Holy Spirit and the words of adjuration, be expelled. You will rightfully command the spirits in others if you have already overcome all their manifold malice in yourself."

"Power over the possessed, baptized or unbaptized", thought Augustine, as he recognized the relationship of this order to that of the office of porter and lector. "By my good example," he resolved, "I must guard the Church on earth, instruct the people of God, and admit new members by freeing them from evil powers." During this reverie his mind darted to Africa, with its vast population of uncatechized people.

"Let those come forward who are to be ordained to the office of acolyte." Augustine's *"Adsum"*, eager and earnest, showed that he was looking forward to the higher duties of this fourth minor order. The symbols—candlestick and cruet—with the commission to light the lights in the church and minister wine and water for the Eucharist, assured him that his place now was beside the officiating priest at the altar, close to the Eternal High Priest. The admonition of Cardinal Parocchi, "Be fervent in all justice and goodness and truth, that you may enlighten yourselves and others", most probably linked themselves in Augustine's mind with Paul's words, "In the midst of a crooked and perverse generation, shine as lights in the world."

On Sunday, August 2, 1885, Augustine Tolton received the first of the three major orders; namely, the subdiaconate. After his *"Adsum"*, he presented himself before the altar, carrying the dalmatic and maniple on his left arm and holding a lighted candle in his right hand. He was deeply aware that this order was one of a higher level and a step closer to the priesthood.

The ordinands listened attentively as Cardinal Parocchi read the canonical message: "Again and again you must carefully consider the office for which you ask of your own accord. For as yet you are free; if you so desire, you may lawfully pass over to secular pursuits; but after you have received this order, you will no longer be free to withdraw from your chosen course, but bound for life to the service of God, to serve whom is to rule. And you will be under obligation to observe celibacy and to employ yourselves in the ministry of the Church at all times. Therefore, while there is time, reflect. If you desire to persevere in your holy resolve, come forward in the name of the Lord."

Augustine Tolton took the irrevocable step.

After the prostration (a symbolic admission of their utter nothingness which the candidates make by prostrating themselves on the floor of the sanctuary), during which the Litany of the Saints was chanted, the candidates received the symbols of their office. Augustine laid his finger upon the chalice, the paten, the cruets, and joyfully accepted the amice emblematic of fruitful works; the dalmatic, a sign of gladness in God's service; and the book of Epistles, a reminder of his obligation to spread Christianity. "In your holy temple," prayed the cardinal, "make them valiant and watchful sentinels of the heavenly army, faithful ministers of thy holy altars."

Again and again during the solemn service, Augustine found himself thinking of the Church in Africa. He saw multitudes of black people ready to receive the Gospel of Christ; he saw himself preaching and celebrating Mass in the vast continent; he saw himself there—a missionary priest.

Long before Augustine Tolton was ordained deacon, he was profoundly impressed by the preeminence of this second major order. He understood that it had a sacramental character, that it conferred special powers and graces; he knew that deacons belonged to the hierarchy of the Church.

After the epistle of the Mass on November 8, 1885, Augustine and the other ordinands presented themselves before the cardinal. Augustine's "*Adsum*", in response to the canonical call, expressed his total dedication. Vested in alb, cincture, amice, and maniple, he carried the stole and dalmatic on the left arm and a lighted candle in the right hand. "Consider well to what exalted rank you rise in the Church", said Cardinal Parocchi. "The office of a deacon is to assist at the altar, to baptize and preach. It is your duty to uphold and defend this Church with the armor of holiness, by divine preaching and good example. Be clean and undefiled, pure and chaste as it behooves ministers of Christ and dispensers of the mysteries of God."

Fully convinced that his future priestly duties lay in Africa, Augustine related every admonition, prayer, and ceremony to the missionary life. Everything he heard on the day he became a deacon seemed to refer to his future duties in the country he had learned to love—Africa. "Receive the Holy Spirit unto power and resist the devil", exhorted the cardinal, laying his hand upon the head of the candidate. "Fulfill your ministry and be clothed with the vesture of gladness and justice", he continued as he imposed the stole and vested the candidate with the dalmatic. Finally, while Augustine's hand lay upon the Gospels, the cardinal concluded, "Receive the power to read the Gospel in the Church of God."

A passage from the closing prayer of the liturgy, "may they scatter the works of your will throughout the universe", heightened the desire of the newly ordained deacon to scatter the word of God far and wide in the dark continent.

"The day I was ordained deacon," Augustine told his confrères in later years, "I felt so strong that I thought no hardship would ever be too great for me to accept. I was ready for anything; in fact, I was very sure I could move mountains—in Africa."

Early in the year 1886, Augustine learned that he would be ordained on Holy Saturday, April 24, and that the ceremony would take place in Saint John Lateran Church, the cathedral of Rome and "mother and head of all churches in Rome and in the world".

*Saint John Lateran Church, where Father
Tolton was ordained April 24, 1886*

During his earlier visits to this cathedral, Augustine had
often stood spellbound before the majestic facade. He admired the magnificent exteriors and the marvelous interior;
the nave with its four aisles and statues, the Cosmati mo-
saics, the canopied papal altar in the center of the transept,
the chapels and shrines, stately columns and choir. Every
time Augustine visited this church his whole being stirred
in anticipation of the coming Holy Saturday. The time came
when he began to count the months, then the weeks, and
finally the days that still remained before he became a priest
and a missionary in Africa. During the final months, as he
took his turn in the seminary chapel as reader of the Epistles and Gospels or as assistant to the officiating priest, he
already experienced some of the joys of the priestly office.
"My seminary studies are about over now," he wrote in his

letter to Father Richardt, "and I will go on to Africa right after my ordination in April."

On Good Friday, April 23, 1886, the day before his ordination, Augustine Tolton's faith was put to a test. On that occasion Cardinal Giovanni Simeoni addressed the assembled deacons. "Each one of you", reminded the cardinal, "has already taken the "Propaganda Oath" which binds you to obedience and fealty; because you are students of the pontifical college you must go wherever you are sent by papal decision."

Augustine nodded his head approvingly as the speaker continued: "Today you must take another oath, namely, to remain in the country and diocese for which you will be ordained. Permission to go elsewhere may be granted only by the Sacred Congregation of the Propagation of the Faith."

It was certainly understood, and from the very beginning, that Augustine Tolton, the American Negro, was destined to go to Africa. He had gained admittance to the papal college through the efforts of Father Bernardin, superior general of the Franciscan Order, and on the ground that he was willing and eager to serve as a missionary in Africa.

Before the time set for the deacons to sign the final oath, Augustine spoke with Cardinal Parocchi. "I know I am going to Africa, Your Eminence," he said with a happy smile, "but can you tell me to which diocese or province I will be assigned?"

"It was our intention all along, Gus", answered the cardinal. "Even in our last meeting most of the members thought that you would not go back to your diocese in America. It seems we have no contact with your American bishop. We all agreed that since you are the only priest of your race in that country, you would perhaps not succeed very well. Then just before the meeting closed Cardinal Simeoni had this idea: 'America needs black priests. America has been called the most enlightened nation. We will see whether it deserves that honor. If the United States has never seen a black priest, it must see one now.' Then we all felt that Cardinal Simeoni was right. Come now, Gus, and sign the oath that you will spend the rest of your life in the United States of America, in the Illinois diocese."

Augustine Tolton took the oath.

It was a crushing blow. And it had come with terrifying swiftness. Augustine was forced to take his bitter disappointment to him who of old asked his apostles: "Can you drink the cup with me?" At his first chance, Augustine stole out of the lecture hall and down the dark stairs and unlighted halls which led to the seminary chapel. In the stillness of that dimly lighted place he fell on his knees before the divine High Priest. He bowed his head and covered his face with his hands: "Back to America? Back to the country where I was a slave, an outcast, a hated black? Must I go back to America, where I was not wanted as a priest? Where seminaries and religious orders were not 'ready'? Lord, I can conquer ignorance, weakness, and heathenism. But Lord, I cannot conquer the racial hatred in America." Tears of anguish trickled through his fingers.

"Can I drink the cup with you, Lord?" Then the thought of tomorrow's ordination to the priesthood raised his spirits and prompted his answer: "I can! Lord, how dare I deny you anything—you who have given me everything? I can drink the cup with you. I want to be a priest. I want to be a priest—in America."

Holy Saturday, April 24, 1886, the day of Augustine's ordination, dawned at last. Pope Leo XIII, Bishop of Rome, delegated Cardinal Giovanni Parocchi to officiate at the ceremony. Members of the clergy, men and women religious and laity—the pious, the spirited, and the curious—came to attend the awe-inspiring rite of ordination in the cathedral of Rome. The deacons, Augustine among them, led by a cross-bearer, entered the basilica in procession and stood before the altar. Cardinal Parocchi's call rang out above the crowd:

"Let those come forward who are to be ordained to the order of priesthood. Augustine Tolton."

"*Adsum*", responded Augustine in a loud, joy-filled voice as he took a quick step ahead.

Throughout the ceremony of this third major order Augustine was overwhelmed with different emotions: first a sense of unworthiness during the prostration, then moments of ecstatic joy. As Cardinal Parocchi and the assisting clergy imposed hands, Augustine realized that a wonderful transformation had taken place. He was an *alter Christus*, a priest forever. He accepted the stole, the sweet yoke of the Lord; he received the chasuble, a symbol of charity. His hands were anointed—a sign of his dedication to the service of God.

"Receive the power to offer sacrifice to God and to celebrate Mass", said the cardinal, as Augustine held the chalice containing wine and water and the paten with the host. He realized that when he said the words of Consecration with the officiating cardinal, he actually celebrated Mass for the first time. "I am a priest now," he thought, "a black priest —the only one in the United States."

With the cardinal's words, "Receive the Holy Spirit, whose sins you shall forgive, they are forgiven them", the newly ordained priest received the second power of the priesthood.

Then with his folded hands between those of the cardinal, Father Augustine Tolton promised obedience to his ecclesiastical superiors. In accordance with their directions he would offer sacrifice, bless, govern, preach, and baptize.

"I will not now call you servants, but friends." Augustine was still reflecting upon these shattering words of Christ himself, repeated by Cardinal Parocchi, as in the procession he and the other new priests moved out of the cathedral. People from all directions hurried toward them. Today the dignitaries and higher clergy went by unnoticed; instead the crowds singled out the newly ordained priests and fell on their knees before them. Among the freshly anointed hands laid upon their heads in blessing were those of Father Augustine Tolton, the American ex-slave.

Saint Peter's Basilica

The next day, Easter Sunday, April 25, 1886, throngs of worshipers and pilgrims present in Saint Peter's Basilica, Rome, witnessed an unusual scene. A temporary altar ordinarily used only by cardinals and distinguished prelates had been erected in the center of the sanctuary.

Father Augustine Tolton

Cardinal Simeoni, always his special friend and counselor, had made arrangements to have Father Tolton celebrate his first Mass at this special altar. In full red-robed regalia, the cardinal took his place beside Augustine as he offered the Mass.

Augustine Tolton's *Introibo altare Dei*, which he had learned from Sister Chrysologus years ago and recited timidly in Quincy's humble Saint Peter's Church, before a sprinkling of worshipers, was on this day wafted up to the vaulted ceiling of the magnificent Saint Peter's Basilica in Rome—the glorious center of Christendom.

Joy and gratitude tinged with poignant memories found

expression in that day's liturgy: "This is the day which the Lord has made; let us rejoice and be glad, for the goodness of the Lord endures forever."

Thus Cardinal Simeoni provided a fitting, even significant close for his friend's life in Rome. There over the tomb of Saint Peter, Father Augustine Tolton ended his preparation and accepted his unique apostolate as America's black priest.

16

A MISSIONARY TO AMERICA

"Father Augustine Tolton, United States of America, diocese of Alton, Illinois." An expression of pain flitted across Augustine's face when he heard the official announcement.

During the Easter season of 1886, Pope Leo XIII received the newly ordained priests of the pontifical college, Father Tolton among them, in private audience. He imparted his benediction as he placed his hand upon the head of each young man kneeling before him.

On the following Ascension Thursday, a simple and impressive chapel ceremony in the pontifical seminary marked the departure of the new priests. A missionary cross, blessed by the Pope, was presented to each priest as the prefect of the Sacred Congregation formally announced the name and destination of each missionary. In his final message Cardinal Simeoni bade the priests farewell, gave them his blessing, and wished them Godspeed on their apostolate "in whatever corner of the Lord's vineyard they happened to labor". The departure service ended with benediction and papal blessing.

True to his promise, Father Francis Ostrop, now stationed in Carlinville, Illinois, had been sending Augustine pocket money regularly during the six years of the seminarian's stay in Rome. But while making arrangements for his journey back to America, Father Tolton discovered that with all his skimping and saving, he still lacked the full amount of money for the passage. He appealed to Cardinal Simeoni, and he in turn submitted the matter to the Sacred Congregation *de Propaganda Fide.*

"Father Augustine Tolton", he wrote, "is now about to leave for Alton, Illinois, his diocese in America. Although he is not profoundly learned, he is nevertheless trustworthy and willing, alert, and obedient", the letter began. Then the writer got to the point: "May it please Your Eminence to allow 220 lires to pay for the journey to America. The amount he already has (485 lire) is not sufficient" (letter dated June 3, 1886, archives of Urban College).

Father Tolton encountered a second difficulty: the ship for his ocean voyage was delayed. Consequently he stayed at the papal seminary until June 13, 1886—seven weeks after the official departure ceremony.

Before he left, Cardinal Simeoni had exacted his promise that he write a letter giving an account of his homeward trip and of his reception in America. Father Tolton complied with the request as is proved by the following excerpt: "I left Rome on the day of Pentecost. With two other passengers I traveled to Civitavecchia. The next day when the ship arrived we sailed for Livorno. As I left the vessel while it lay in anchor, an Italian immigration officer accosted me and wanted me to enlist, that is, take service on a warship. I refused, of course, and went back to our ship. The officer followed me on board and begged me again. When I told him that I was an American he immediately refrained from further prodding. This officer was under the impression that I was an Italian subject from Massaua because I spoke Italian. When we arrived at Marseilles, France, I, with other passengers, was put under quarantine for some unknown reason. We were released after twenty-four hours."

At the close of the letter Father Tolton promised the cardinal that he would write again when he reached America.

Then Father Tolton had an unexpected, yet pleasant experience. An Irish gentleman, most likely attracted by the Roman collar and clerical suit, approached the priest at Southampton, England, just as both of them were leaving the ship. The Irish gentleman, whose name is not known, greeted the priest warmly. Together they made inquiries concerning passage to the United States and learned that no vessel would leave port for another twelve days. True to the tradition of his countrymen, the stranger went out of his way to help the priest. He offered to pay the expenses of a tour through parts of England and Europe as a mark of esteem for "his reverence". Father Tolton gladly accepted the offer. They crossed the channel, and while in Europe the Irish gentleman made arrangements for Father Tolton's celebration of Mass in several famous churches. They visited several cities and saw many historical landmarks. Upon their return to England they followed a similar program. Finally they went to the port of Liverpool, where Father Tolton boarded the *Cunarder Gallia*, which arrived in New York on July 6, 1886.

Father Augustine's first act as an American priest was to fulfill the promise he had made to Sister Perpetua in Hoboken, six years earlier—that if he ever returned to the United States, he would celebrate Mass in her hospital chapel. Accordingly, on the morning of July 7, 1886, the day after his arrival in New York, he offered Mass before the assembled Franciscan community. He was assisted by Father John Corrigan, chaplain of the hospital.

Sister Perpetua and her colleagues not only rejoiced on the day Father Augustine Tolton fulfilled his promise but for the benefit of their community they recorded the fact: "The first Mass in the United States by the first African-American priest and ex-slave was celebrated on Wednesday, July 7, 1886, in the chapel of Saint Mary's Hospital of Hoboken."

On February 15, 1886, Peter J. Baltes, bishop of Alton, had died—less than two months before the ordination of Father Tolton. The administrator was Father John Janssen, vicar general, who in 1877–1879 had been pastor of Saint Boniface Church in Quincy. In June of 1886, he received a communication from the prefect of the Sacred Congregation *de Propaganda Fide*, Cardinal Giovanni Parocchi. The writer stated, "Father Augustine Tolton of Quincy, Illinois, was ordained to the priesthood on April 24. He is assigned to the diocese of Alton in Illinois. Upon his arrival in your city he will call on you to present his credentials. He will most likely land in New York early next month.

"We have advanced 220 lires which Father Tolton needed to pay for his voyage, and we have charged this amount to the diocese of Alton. Father Tolton is a good priest, reliable, worthy, and capable. You will discover that he is deeply spiritual and dedicated" (letter dated June 16, 1886, archives of Urban College).

Father Tolton wanted to celebrate his first solemn High Mass in America in a black parish and did so at Saint Benedict the Moor Church, located at Bleeker and Downing Streets in New York City, July 11, 1886, in the presence of a vast crowd of black worshipers. The whole scene—a black celebrant with a white priest on either side—is graphically described in the *New York World*, July 12, 1886: Long before the hour fixed, every seat in the church of Saint Benedict the Moor was filled; black people, old and young, came from all parts of the city and many from out of town.

*Father Tolton celebrated his first Mass in the United States
in the chapel of Saint Mary's Hospital of Hoboken, New Jersey*

The presence of the black priest in the church caused all
eyes to be turned on him, and every one of his actions was
watched.

He was perfectly at ease and sang the Mass in a powerful

voice which filled the whole church. He was a fine-looking man, nearly six feet in height.

He was assisted by the pastor of Saint Benedict the Moor Church, as deacon, and by Father Thomas O'Keefe, as sub-deacon. The sermon was given by the Reverend D. Burtsell, rector of Epiphany College.

As soon as the exact date of Father Tolton's arrival in Quincy was known, plans and preparations were made by priests and townspeople of that city for a fitting homecoming.

Father McGirr began a month in advance. "We must make it nice for Gus", he told Sister Herlinde. Soon the whole parish was enthusiastic, eager to give Father Tolton what they called "a proper reception". Father McGirr, an integrationist to the core, wanted to prove to everyone— the people of his town, of his state, and the whole United States—that blacks could succeed. Above all, he wanted it to be known that such success is possible because the Church makes no distinction of race, color, or nationality. Now he had a chance to prove it.

"We will charter a special railroad car to meet him at Springfield", Father McGirr told some of the other priests of Quincy. "We'll head a delegation of Negro and white people, with Mrs. Tolton and Anne, of course, to welcome him and accompany him home."

As the train pulled into the Quincy station, a brass band played "Holy God, we praise thy name". The large crowd that had assembled at the depot waved and cheered as the priest was escorted toward a flower-draped carriage drawn by four white horses. The band marched ahead of the procession as it moved toward Saint Peter's Church and played decidedly black ethnic music while the crowd shouted, "Father Tolton, Father Augustine Tolton. Welcome home! Welcome home!"

At the church the procession was met by school children, sisters, more priests, and more people. When Father Tolton took his place in the sanctuary, hundreds of people came to the Communion railing to receive his first blessing. Before approaching the others Father Augustine Tolton laid his hands in benediction on the head of his mother.

Father McGirr had agreed with Father Bruener, who was still the pastor there, that spacious Saint Boniface Church was the proper place for Father Tolton's first solemn Mass in Quincy. A second reason for this choice was found in the fact that the already established black parish, Saint Joseph's, owed its existence mainly to the efforts and cooperation of Saint Boniface parish—first in its form as a day school and later as a parish and center for black schooling and worship.

On July 18, 1886, Father Tolton celebrated his first Mass in Quincy. Hours before the scheduled time, 11:00 A.M., every seat in the church was taken, and lines of worshipers stood in the aisles. Everyone—white and black, Catholics and non-Catholics—wanted to see and hear the black priest. They wanted to hear his melodious voice at the altar and his address to the congregation; they wanted to congratulate him upon his extraordinary success—his elevation to the priesthood.

Father Theodore Bruener, then dean, made this observation: "The celebration of Father Augustine Tolton's first Mass was in our church, where as a boy he served Mass. The crowd was larger than we ever had before for any occasion. The children of the parish had been told to attend an early Mass, and none were permitted to come to the solemn Mass simply because there was no room. Despite that, the church was filled to capacity. In the gallery as well as in the aisles right up to the altar, all standing room was taken. Some had to remain outside.

"The Reverend George Pesch, assistant priest at Saint Boniface, was deacon; the Reverend Maurice Baukolt, O.F.M., was subdeacon; the Reverend Boniface Depmann, O.F.M., was master of ceremonies; and the Reverend Peter McGirr was archpriest. The Reverend Anselm Mueller, O.F.M., rector of Quincy College, gave the sermon."

The choir, directed by Mr. Oscar Hueck, sang "Missa Stabat Mater" by John Singenberger.

After the Mass Father Tolton addressed the congregation. In his simple yet eloquent manner, he gave public thanks to God for his vocation to the priesthood. Then he expressed his gratitude to his many benefactors—people, sisters, priests. And finally, in a voice trembling with emotion as he looked at Mrs. Tolton, who was in the first pew, he said, "Above all, I want to thank my mother."

True to his promise to Cardinal Checchi—namely, that he would write as soon as he reached his diocese and had an assignment—Father Tolton wrote a letter in September 1886, which states in part, "In America everyone received me kindly, especially the Negroes but also the white people: Germans, Irish, and all others. I celebrated Mass on July 18, in the Church of Saint Boniface with more than 1,000 whites and 500 colored people present. After the Mass all shouted, 'Hail to the Propaganda College; long live the College in Rome.'

"The episcopal administrator, the Reverend John Janssen, received me kindly and even joyfully; he appointed me pastor of the Negro Church of Saint Joseph in Quincy, Illinois."

17

FATHER TOLTON, PASTOR

On July 25, 1886, Father Augustine Tolton was formally installed as pastor of Saint Joseph's parish. As a sign of his authority and his responsibility for the spiritual welfare of the parish, a key to the church was presented to Father Tolton by Father Janssen, administrator of the diocese. Observing the rite of installation, the episcopal delegate escorted the pastor to the altar, to the confessional, and to the pulpit: customary ceremonies that symbolize the duties of celebrating Mass, forgiving sins, and proclaiming the word of God.

All the places in the small church were reserved for members of the parish. Crowds of white people, waiting outside the church to congratulate him as pastor, could hear the sermon given by Father Bruener of Saint Boniface as he traced the history of Saint Joseph's parish and recalled the day school organized by Father Michael Richardt in 1878 —a project in which Father Tolton, as we have seen, had played such a vital role as recruiter and assistant teacher. He extolled the self-sacrificing service of Sister Herlinde and the consequent success of the school; he described the disappointment experienced by everyone in 1881 when the Franciscan Provincial ordered the school to be closed.

Then the speaker gave a glowing account of the reopening of Saint Joseph's in 1883, with both a church and a school. He touched upon the hardships that the priests from the

Saint Joseph's Church, Quincy

three parishes endured because of their zeal and determination to minister to the black congregation and the fact that, because of the shortage of clerical assistants, the service at Saint Joseph's during the past year had to be reduced to a low Mass two days of the week and only vespers and catechetical instruction on Sunday. Then he referred to the vocation and mission of Father Tolton as an unmistakable sign of God's providence. He emphasized this statement by informing the people that Bishop Baltes had given permission just before his death to close the church because no priest was available at the time.

With the coming of a resident pastor, adequate opportunities for divine service would be offered again, concluded Father Bruener. He congratulated Father Tolton and called God's blessing upon him and his flock. Finally, he exhorted the parishioners to support the new pastor by their loyalty and cooperation.

Father Tolton began his duties with the exuberance characteristic of the newly ordained. Following the precedent of Sunday worship programs set by other parishes in Quincy, he offered an early low Mass and a midmorning high Mass. He preached at both Masses and conducted vespers with Benediction and catechetical instruction in the afternoon.

After Mass each weekday, Father Tolton taught Bible history and catechism in the parish school. Not only the children but also Sister Herlinde were elated at their "good fortune", as they called it. Father Tolton scheduled convert classes and counseling for the afternoon and evening. Whenever time permitted, he visited the homes of parishioners, especially, those of the aged and the sick; he made tireless efforts to gain new members for his parish and children for the school.

From the outset Father Tolton realized that he faced grave,

if not insurmountable, difficulties; he knew that complex moral problems and serious irregularities existed among his people and that outside factors were unfavorable to the spiritual progress of his parish.

Father Bruener, a leading force among the founders of Saint Joseph's Church and School, wrote a detailed account of the situation in his *Kirchengeschichte Quincy's*. Because Father Bruener was a contemporary of Father Tolton and a daily witness of his adversities as well as of his desperate efforts in behalf of his race, his record is transcribed in English here:

> Special recognition must be given to Mrs. Joseph Ducker, the former Caecilia Schwab, for her efforts in enriching divine service. As a girl she had the privilege of studying music at the local sisters' convent. Expecting no remuneration, she accepted the position of organist and choir leader in Saint Joseph's Church. She trained a choir of Negro and white girls and practiced the necessary liturgical singing. But more than that, she practiced patience. A small Christmas gift was all that could be given her as recompense, and in recent years she did not even accept that. May God reward her! At first Mrs. Ducker had to manage both choir and organ in the body of the church just behind the last pews, but later a gallery was constructed by Mr. Ducker at the cost of $100.00. This "integrated" choir, which lasted as long as the parish, gives proof of the absolute absence of racial prejudice. Weekly rehearsals were held in the school or in the home of Mrs. Ducker.

"The church itself, which measures 36 feet by 70 feet," continued Father Bruener, "was beautifully decorated by Mr. Henry Gantert and at a reasonable cost. Pictures of the Stations of the Cross, done in oil, adorn the walls. To the left of the high altar is a shrine with a statue of the Blessed

Virgin Mary and on the right side is a similar shrine with a statue of Saint Joseph.

"The prescribed liturgical vestments were purchased from the Herder Company of Saint Louis at the cost of $112.00."

Further evidence of amicable race relations is found in the existence and growth of Saint Joseph's Altar Society. The organization of forty-eight members had been founded before the coming of Father Tolton. Eventually the membership increased and consisted of eighty black and white women. During its regular meetings the society worked effectively toward the material upkeep of the parish. Through group interest and cooperation substantial sums were raised to help maintain the church and school.

The people, white and black, provided generously for the personal needs of Father Tolton. With his mother as housekeeper and sacristan, he lived in one part of the so-called Old Seminary[1] located on the southeast corner of Eighth and Main Streets. A kind friend, one Mr. Mast, paid the rent and maintained the building.

The record of Father Bruener continues, "Every Sunday the church is filled to capacity. Father Tolton, the first Negro priest from America, is highly esteemed by all, and everyone likes to listen to his sermons."

Quite abruptly the account of Saint Joseph's parish takes on a strange new tone. The parish, it is conceded, lacks solidarity and actual progress.

All of this would be well and good if only there were a parish. The well-disposed reader knows that for the past ten years

[1] The "Old Seminary" was the first Franciscan friary in Quincy. The pioneer priests lived in this three-story building until the new Saint Francis Friary was built. In recent years a memorial has been erected to mark the historical site.

much has been done for the conversion of the Negroes in Quincy; the results, however, are almost nil. The only real success is found in the baptism of several infants which certainly would not have happened otherwise—infants who died soon afterward. Several converts were made who did persevere in the faith. But as a whole in terms of achievement the Negro mission has absolutely not paid off. If matters do not improve within the next year, Father Tolton must shake the dust from his feet and look for a more rewarding field elsewhere. To most of the Negroes in Quincy one could say with absolute truth, "Jerusalem, Jerusalem! Thou wouldst not." Many will ask the question: "What is the reason for this?" The school was always well attended—actually many children were baptized.

In the final part of his account Father Bruener endeavors to explain the underlying causes of the parish's weakness and instability. "Dire poverty always has a demoralizing effect," he begins, "and moral depravity in some homes defies description."

Sister Herlinde and her companion soon found out that the children were very poor. In fact, some of them were destitute. It was only because they received clothing and shoes, sometimes even food, that they came to school at all. Catholic as well as non-Catholic children crowded into the classrooms in winter just to have a warm place. An excerpt from Father Bruener's account is further proof that the children came from disorganized homes:

> Just yesterday Father Tolton told me that in the course of the year nine different men came to see him because they were inclined toward becoming Catholic but would do so only under the condition that they would be permitted to retain their present "wife"! Actually each one had another wife elsewhere. To most of the women one can say, as the

Lord Jesus did at Jacob's well, "The one you have now is not
your husband."

Father Tolton's work as a pastor was constantly impeded
by the activities of churchmen representing non-Catholic
denominations. They made their services so attractive to
the blacks, the old and the young, that many of these were
led away from the Catholic Church. "At the nightly religious services," says Father Bruener, "sensuality is stimu-
lated through song and dance. This usually happens at their
so-called revivals and camp meetings (assemblies of both
sexes under the same tent for as long as eight days). No
wonder that the minds and hearts of uneducated Negroes
join them, and the more so because they have an innate in-
clination toward rhythmic music and dances."

It is true that of the sixty or more pupils—the average
school attendance—many had been baptized or were under
instruction. Father Tolton and the sisters hoped that they
would eventually win the parents through these young converts. However, in too many instances this did not material-
ize. Because of disrupted family life, indifferent or careless
adults, and the far greater attraction of other denominations,
the school got no hold on the family, but, on the contrary,
the family influence proved detrimental to the school. Father Bruener gives a typical example:

> Now just think of a girl fourteen to sixteen years of age. She
> attended school regularly and received her first Holy Com-
> munion. Her parents, brothers, and sisters are Methodists.
> What should she do when the exciting revivals are taking
> place? All her companions attend them, and if she wishes to
> keep away, her relatives and friends ridicule her for her Cath-
> olic bigotry. A young man comes along and enticingly offers
> her his arm—will she not go along? In every ten cases, nine

will certainly acquiesce. And if the girl does go along, she is
as good as lost to the Church.

Since this was a common occurrence, it is not hard to believe that Sister Herlinde and her companion, and certainly
Father Tolton, were thoroughly disheartened.

Added to this was the problem of secret societies, which
always presented obstacles to the propagation of Catholicism. Father Tolton was aware of the fact that children at
the age of ten, boys and girls, held membership and were
periodically promoted. He knew how the subtle tactics of
these organizations enchained black children and young people and at times robbed them completely of their Catholic
training.

Father Bruener injects a bit of grim humor into the dismal
picture he described:

> Deplorable as this situation is, we can not refrain from re-
> lating a witticism with which the mother of Father Tolton
> silenced a Baptist minister. This religious leader made the
> reproach that Catholics lured children to Sunday School and
> to church, simply by giving them everything for nothing, and
> then added, "In the end they all go to hell anyway." "Well,
> Dean," retorted Mrs. Tolton, "if the Catholics all go to hell,
> then hell will soon be filled up; but as soon as you Baptists
> come we will move out and make room for you; we Catholics
> are charitable people."

It must not be understood that there were no faithful
members in Father Tolton's parish. On the contrary, there
were a considerable number of loyal and courageous blacks
who attended divine worship regularly and received the
sacraments. But Father Tolton was concerned about *all* members of his parish.

Despite the day-after-day frustrations that dogged his footsteps, the pastor conscientiously performed his duties; he continued to be zealous and hopeful.

The constant presence of white people in his congregation gave Father Tolton strength and courage. Even though he was aware that some of them attended merely for the novel experience of seeing a black priest, he knew that there were others who came to fulfill their obligations and profit by his sermons. It was very common to see white people in the line of penitents outside his confessional. Since most of the blacks of his parish were desperately poor and therefore unable to support the church and school, Father Tolton was of course heartened by the generous contributions made by white worshipers; but the fact that blacks and whites knelt side by side, that there was no indication of racial prejudice in Saint Joseph's parish, must have given him far greater pleasure and satisfaction.

In his first report to the Sacred Congregation *de Propaganda Fide*, dated July 25, 1887, Father Tolton's attitude is expressed:

> During the year that I have been pastor the number of Negro Catholics has not increased. It seems they do not care much for religion. The majority of Negroes in this place are Baptists and Calvinists; many of them are Masons. I had only six converts this year.
>
> The Negroes in Chicago, Illinois, complain that I am here in Quincy and that they do not have a Negro priest. They have asked Archbishop Feehan of Chicago to appeal to Rome for my transfer to Chicago. One of the priests here also tells me that I am wasting my time in Quincy.
>
> Your Eminence, please advise me whether I should ask to leave here or whether I should stay. The German and Irish people have helped me generously by supporting the parish, and they too want me to remain here.

In the neighboring parishes people are making money by selling my picture. This is being done without my consent and with my expressed displeasure and objections.

I have also been asked to travel and give lectures in various cities in order to earn money for the parish. I refused to do this without the permission and consent of the Sacred Congregation. I am contented to work here in Quincy.

In the letter of reply dated August 29, 1887, the cardinal prefect states, "You are giving complete satisfaction. You are doing good work, and we advise you to stay there. You cannot go elsewhere without the consent of the bishop of your diocese. So long as you are in Quincy you are under the jurisdiction of the bishop of Alton."

Father Tolton was encouraged by the reply and resolved to labor even more strenuously at his uphill task, confident that God looked upon his efforts and not the results even though he felt no tangible success. He received encouragement too from some of his fellow priests and from the bishop. They always referred to him as "good Father Gus".

Shortly after Bishop James Ryan was installed as Ordinary of the Alton diocese, Father Tolton made a special trip to the episcopal residence in order to pay his respects. Bishop Ryan had read the recommendations concerning Father Augustine Tolton that the prefect of the Sacred Congregation had sent to the chancery earlier. The document, dated June 4, 1886, states, "Augustine Tolton is endowed with average intelligence. He is a Negro from America and is highly commended for self-sacrifice, piety, and other virtues. He is very capable and especially trained for the discharge of the sacred ministry. However, he seems to be much concerned about what he may experience from the dominant race in America."

Bishop Ryan showed great interest and sincere pleasure in his meeting with the black priest. He welcomed Father Tolton warmly, spoke kindly to him about his parish in Quincy, and imparted his blessing.

18

THE BITTER DRAUGHT

Bishop Ryan soon learned that Father Augustine Tolton was indeed "a good priest, capable and pious, dedicated to the sacred ministry", as the cardinal prefect had written. Everyone admired the zeal that the black priest expended in the cause of his parish; they saw that he braved the future with a stout heart and hopeful outlook.

Father Tolton promptly won the loyalty of the few black members of his congregation. Many blacks outside the Catholic Church were proud of him because he was a priest and easily distinguished from ordinary men by the clerical garb which he usually wore. Father Tolton's outfit was even more distinctive than that of other diocesan priests. The black soutane with red cincture and the black biretta with red tassel indicated that he had been trained in the pontifical seminary in Rome and that he was still allied with the papal household. The many white people who from time to time came to Saint Joseph's Church, perhaps first out of curiosity, were captivated by Father Tolton's inspiring sermons and his beautiful singing.

The Quincy *Journal*, July 26, 1886, describes the priest's ability and accomplishments in phrases such as "his fine educational training", his "oratorical ability", his "rich and full voice which falls pleasantly on the ear", and his "whole-souled earnestness".

The Reverend Stephen Duren's article in the *Interracial Review* of May 1935 expressed admiration for the priest's singing even though he was completely carried away in his attempt to describe the voice and the effect Father Tolton's performance must have had on the congregation.

Constant high acclaim and publicity by the press or through verbal reports were certain to bring more and more white Catholics to Saint Joseph's Church. Many of these people knew Father Tolton as "Gus" or "Augustine", the parish custodian or factory hand whom they had often seen on Quincy's streets. These people now revered him as a priest; they forgot his color and saw no harm in adoring God in the company of black worshipers. The daughters of some white people joined the choir, directed by a white woman. And it was not uncommon to see a white and a black boy serving Mass together.

"The little Church was crowded every Sunday," confirms Marion A. Habig, O.F.M., in his book *Heralds of the King*, "and among them were white Catholics who attended services because they loved to hear him [Father Tolton] preach the word of God."

Tradition has it that whenever Father Tolton noticed adults standing in the rear of the church or in the aisles at the beginning of his sermon, he raised both arms in a beckoning gesture. The children, who understood the sign, scampered forward and sat on the floor, forming semicircles around the preacher. This provided seats for the adults and delight for the children.

Father Tolton won the hearts of old and young alike. The secret of his success lay in his innate simplicity and genuine love for all with whom he came in contact. He never tired of telling his people that God cared for each one of them and that he had a deep concern for the welfare of every one of his children. To prove his statements he invariably referred to the Gospel. By means of a clear explanation or simple dramatization, Father Tolton was able to recreate scenes of Christ's life on earth and his mission among mankind; he repeated the words of the Master with such profound reverence that his hearers sensed the presence of the living Christ. No prelate ever received higher praise than that accorded to Father Tolton by a very young pupil of Saint Joseph's School. Seeing the priest on the street, the child said to its mother, "See, there goes Jesus."

Father Tolton sincerely appreciated the white people who worshiped in Saint Joseph's Church. He knew that they not only helped the parish materially but that they also provided much needed morale. The choir, the evening classes, the parish organizations, and the congregation as a whole were strengthened by interested white Catholics. Saint Joseph's School, however, under the charge of Sister Herlinde and her assistant, was attended by black children only.

Although the coming of Father Tolton promised success for Saint Joseph's parish, it soon became apparent that the favorable signs that characterized his early pastorate rested upon a weak foundation. The priest's first report to the Sacred Congregation *de Propaganda Fide*, "I am very happy here in Quincy", was not destined to last. The forces of destruction were at work; these, as Father Tolton feared, were the Protestant ministers and their adherents. Methodists, Baptists, and Presbyterians had opened churches for blacks in Quincy long before the Catholics provided a place of worship for their black coreligionists. In fact, the first Negro church in Quincy was founded by the Methodists as early as 1852. The Protestants looked askance at the opening of Saint Joseph's Day School in 1877, and they eyed the subsequent development of a church with open alarm. Father Tolton's triumphal return to Quincy after a six-year period of training under papal auspices inflamed many of the non-Catholic leaders with the dread that Protestantism would be conquered through Roman influence. Consequently, unpleasant scenes resulted from efforts by Methodists and Baptists to stay "papal inroads". Churches of other denominations did not want to lose members, and certainly not to the Catholic cause. This attitude was prevalent from the time Saint Joseph's Church and the parochial school were established, but the ill will turned into open indignation when Father Tolton became pastor.

According to Father Bruener's account,

> the wide publicity and munificent praise which heralded the coming of Father Tolton added fuel to the wrath of certain Protestant church leaders. They redoubled their efforts not only to save their own church members from "Romanism", but they also made many efforts to lure Catholics from the fold. Their missionary methods were all too powerful; weak and poorly instructed members of Saint Joseph's parish frequently became the prey of unscrupulous foes of Catholicism.

Father Tolton, who understood the zeal as well as the tenets of non-Catholics, resolved to maintain amicable and respectful relations with all members of other religious persuasions. He respected their convictions and carefully refrained from downgrading their forms of religious worship. He sympathized with them when white people referred to their houses of prayer as "nigger churches" and called their ordained leaders "nigger ministers". He himself, of course, was deeply offended when Saint Joseph's Church became known as the "nigger place" and he identified as "nigger priest". On more than one occasion he appealed to the people of his parish to refrain from using terms which savored of irreverence: "I must remind you", he exhorted, "to honor the house of God; I must beg you to respect the priesthood in me. Do all you can to keep others from debasing the Church and her ministers through insulting language." He told his people that this instruction applied to non-Catholic churches and their ministers as well.

Shortly after this appeal, a young member of the parish, noted for his candor rather than for his prudence, gave Father Tolton this information: "Father Weiss always calls you the 'nigger priest'."

Father Tolton's latent and worst fears were confirmed. "A brother priest", he thought, "harboring ill will toward me? Prejudice? And expressing it openly—in the presence of children?" He tried to dispel the idea, but the whole truth gradually dawned upon him. He recalled that on more than one occasion during the past year he had sensed the coolness, the hostile stare, and the condescending attitude of this German priest.

The sting of prejudice and racial hatred that Father Tolton feared and to which he had been subjected in early childhood and youth did not harass him to any considerable degree during the first year of his ministry in Quincy. Then came the unexpected thrust, the deadly blow. Now added to his other hardships and apparent lack of success as pastor, Father Tolton had to endure the "most unkindest cut of all" —ill will of a brother priest based upon race prejudice.

Father Michael Weiss was appointed pastor of Saint Boniface Church and also ecclesiastical dean in November 1887. Because of his efforts to liquidate the enormous debt of his parish and place it upon a firm financial basis, Father Weiss was known as the "financier of Saint Boniface". Naturally he was unhappy about the generous donations his people made to the black parish. Moreover, he was irked by the constant glowing reports from Saint Joseph's Church: "The wonderful sermons" . . . "the saintly priest" . . . "the kind and consoling words". At that rate, Father Weiss concluded, the black church would always be frequented by white people unless some restraint or control was exercised by authority and worshipers compelled to attend and support the parishes with which they were affiliated.

Father Weiss complained to his congregation that they had supported St. Joseph's parish all too long: ten years earlier, after Father Janssen had donated the very building, they had continued to maintain it, he reminded his people again and again.

On more than one occasion Father Weiss, in no uncertain terms, told Father Tolton that he was expected to minister only to blacks; he told him bluntly that he should order the white people out of his church. Father Tolton replied in a matter-of-fact fashion, "Why, Father, we open the doors to the church. We do not tell people to go *out*; we tell them to go *into* the church." And his friendly smile met with a threatening scowl.

The time came when Father Weiss acted with open hostility. He avowed publicly that the money collected from white people attending Saint Joseph's Church belonged to their own parishes and even insinuated that attendance at the black church was not valid in the case of white Catholics. Father Tolton began to notice the dwindling attendance, and when he confronted his more honest friends, some said they were confused and disillusioned; others maintained that they discontinued attendance for "the sake of peace". Finally, there were those who admitted that they could not endure the designation of "nigger lover".

Whatever other means Father Weiss used to gain his end

have not been fully divulged. Father Tolton's report to Rome simply states, "He is persecuting me." And in a personal letter to a Josephite priest, Father Slattery, he writes, "The facts I have kept hidden and will never let them out through fear of it greatly injuring the success of the mission among the colored race."

Reluctant in the beginning, Father Tolton accepted speaking engagements during the first part of the year 1889 as a means of raising funds to maintain the church and school. Father Foley, S.J., in *God's Men of Color*, makes this observation: "Father Tolton had the strength and courage to overcome the frustrations brought about by his seemingly fruitless labors in his immediate surroundings." If he was the "unaccepted prophet" in Quincy, he was, nevertheless, welcomed and even demanded in other cities.

Leaders of the First Catholic Colored Congress in Washington, D.C., held in 1889, scheduled Father Augustine Tolton as main speaker, introducing him as the first black priest of the United States. At the close of this congress Father Tolton gave Benediction of the Blessed Sacrament to the large number of prominent church and civic leaders.

Cardinal James Gibbons made arrangements to have Father Tolton speak before both blacks and whites in Baltimore. Later Father Tolton gave similar addresses to large audiences in New York and Boston.

He was not afraid to go into the deep South, where racial hatreds had reached a high pitch and where segregation was decreed by harsh laws. At the request of Bishop Gallagher of Galveston, Texas, he preached in the cathedral where the congregation was predominantly white. In this cathedral as well as in the Jesuit church at the east end of the island, next to Saint Mary's University, Father Tolton heard confessions of both white and black penitents. Wherever he went, he was respected and honored.

A portion of the lecture Father Tolton gave to some of his audiences is found in *Our Colored Missions*, June 1945:

> The Catholic Church deplores a double slavery—that of the mind and that of the body. She endeavors to free us of both. I was a poor slave boy, but the priests of the Church did not disdain me. It was through the influence of one of them that I became what I am tonight. I must now give praise to that son of the Emerald Isle, Father Peter McGirr, who promised me that I would be educated and who kept his word. It was the priests of the Church who taught me to pray and to forgive my persecutors.
>
> It was through the direction of a School Sister of Notre Dame, Sister Herlinde, that I learned to interpret the Ten Commandments; and then I also beheld for the first time the glimmering light of truth and the majesty of the Church. I was finally admitted to the College *de Propaganda Fide*, and I found out that I was not the only black man there. There were students from Africa, China, Japan, and other parts of the world.
>
> The Church which knows and makes no distinction in race and color had called them all. When the Church does all of this, is she not a true liberator of the race? In this Church we do not have to fight for our rights because we are black. She had colored saints—Saint Augustine, Saint Benedict the Moor, Saint Monica, the mother of Saint Augustine. The Church is broad and liberal. She is the Church for our people.

With these reflections still in his mind, Father Tolton came back to Quincy and faced the same round of frustrations and humiliations. Before the end of his second year as pastor, he was preaching to vacant pews, to a very small group of loyal white friends and to a black Catholic remnant desperately poor and plainly discouraged. Sister Herlinde and her assistant kept the school open; Father Tolton worked tirelessly for the welfare of the children and for those people who remained in the disintegrated and impoverished parish.

An event with strong repercussions tended to decrease still more of the prestige of Saint Joseph's parish and to cause Father Tolton no small measure of mental anguish. The story is told by Father Landry Genosky, O.F.M., archivist of Quincy College (the former Saint Francis Solano):

> A wealthy Catholic society matron objected to her daughter's marrying an unacceptable person and was able to bring enough pressure to have the doors of Quincy's white churches barred to the white couple. She [the mother] did not figure on Father Tolton. Consequently, one of the wealthiest daughters of Quincy's highest society was married in a Negro church. . . . The society scion never did forget nor forgive him [Father Tolton], nor did she allow him to forget.

But Father Tolton had acted with clerical propriety. Both he and the couple had full permission from Father Weiss that the marriage could take place in Saint Joseph's Church.

This affair together with his other worries did not deter Father Tolton from making repeated efforts toward reaching an understanding with Father Weiss; he made use of every opportunity to gain the friendship and good will of the white priest. On one occasion when Father Tolton humbly asked for advice concerning the parish—which Father Weiss as dean was in a position to give—he received sharp orders to go elsewhere if he was not able to manage his own affairs.

"I may not go elsewhere. I am bound by the *Propaganda Oath*, which obliges me to go only where the church authorities send me," explained Father Tolton, "and since I have been appointed to this parish, I must remain."

"Well, then, I'll take up the matter with the bishop", answered Father Weiss. "Bishop Ryan can send you to some other diocese."

After Father Weiss, who, as Father Landry Genosky, O.F.M. states, "was powerful with the bishop", had conferred with Bishop Ryan, Father Tolton was summoned to the office of the chancery at Alton. He was sternly admonished to heed the advice of the dean of Quincy and to refrain from luring white worshipers away from other parishes. He was told to minister to black people only or to go elsewhere.

Because the bishop had issued the ultimatum, Father Tolton could not appeal to the other priests in Quincy, all of whom were his friends. Father Weiss, who had won the day, brought more and more pressure upon the white people by publicizing Bishop Ryan's mandate.

Now Father Tolton, who was completely distraught, began to think about making an appeal to Rome. Before making a final decision he made inquiries about an opening for him in other dioceses where black missions had been opened.

The reason he was not accepted by Archbishop Ireland of Saint Paul is stated in a letter dated September 13, 1888, which James L. Byrne, secretary of the archdiocese, wrote to Father John Slattery, superior of the Josephites in Baltimore:

Father Tolton of Quincy, Illinois, the colored priest, has written to His Grace asking to come to Saint Paul. Archbishop Ireland is not ready yet to go any deeper into his funds for the colored missions here. The poor Negro priest is sent from pillar to post it seems, and no one appears to help him or give him a guiding hand. Of course, I have written, at His

Grace's dictation, to the poor man telling him to write to
you for information. The archbishop suggests that he [Father
Tolton] should work under your direction.

Father Tolton's first letter to the cardinal prefect of the Sacred Congregation *de Propaganda Fide*, dated July 12, 1889,
contained a complete account of his situation in Quincy.
The following is an excerpt: "There is a certain German
priest here who is jealous and contemptuous. He abuses me
in many ways, and he has told the bishop to send me out of
this place. I will gladly leave here just to be away from this
priest. . . . I appealed to Bishop Ryan, and he also advises
me to go elsewhere."

Because the Sacred Congregation found it necessary in
the cause of justice to make a thorough investigation of the
case, Father Tolton received no immediate reply.

A letter dated August 5, 1889, addressed to Bishop Ryan
of Alton, by the cardinal prefect of the Sacred Congregation, states in part, "We have received a letter of request
from Father Augustine Tolton of your diocese. He asks to
be missioned to a different diocese. Please give us the reasons why Father Tolton makes this request."

Bishop Ryan's reply, dated August 20, 1889, was incred-
ibly brief and unconvincing: "Father Augustine Tolton is a
good priest. However, he wants to establish a type of society here which is not feasible in this place." (This information was so vague and evasive that the archivist of the Urban College, Father Joseph Pallikaparampil, was prompted
to add this comment: "He does not say anything else and
appears to answer little to the point.")

After Father Tolton received word that there was no opening for him in the archdiocese of Saint Paul, he wrote to
Archbishop Patrick Feehan of Chicago. The letter he re-

ceived in reply assured Father Tolton of a warm welcome; he was told that there was an urgent need for his service as the pastor of Chicago's black Catholics.

But Father Tolton had no word from Rome. He believed that his first letter had not reached its destination, and so, on September 4, 1889, he appealed to the cardinal prefect of the Sacred Congregation a second time: "I beg you to give me permission to go to the diocese of Chicago", he wrote. "It is not possible for me to remain here any longer with this German priest. My bishop gives his consent."

After waiting for a long time with still no word from the Sacred Congregation, Father Tolton made a third attempt on October 7, 1889.

> The bishop appreciated my work, but he told me that this is not the right place for me, and he has advised me to go elsewhere. Bishop Feehan of Chicago has invited me to come to his diocese if the bishop of Alton would give his consent. The bishop of Chicago has asked me to request this permission of Your Eminence.
>
> There are nineteen Negroes here whom I have baptized, and they will follow me to Chicago. I think I will go at once as soon as I receive your consent. I anticipate that you will let me go. I wish to go on account of this German priest who continually treats me with harshness. However, the black people as well as the white people like me very much.

Father Tolton received the long-awaited consent on December 7, 1889. The cardinal prefect wrote, "If the two bishops concur in giving their approval, that is sufficient. In that case further permission from the Sacred Congregation is not necessary for your transfer to the diocese of Chicago. Just go at once."

Bishop Ryan received his version of the approval on the

same day: "Augustine Tolton has asked the Sacred Congregation to permit him to go to Chicago. Such a permission is not required; the consent of the respective ecclesiastical superiors suffices."

It was December 19, 1889, when Father Tolton left Quincy—the parish of the diocese to which he had been assigned by the Sacred Congregation *de Propaganda Fide*, on April 23, 1886.

He preferred to leave Quincy without the excitement and publicity of farewells. Only a few close friends besides his mother and sister were informed. He sent his few personal effects ahead. People who saw him at the railway station surmised that he was going on a speaking tour.

And now as he leaned back wearily in the seat of the Jim Crow coach, he knew he had not succeeded; some had called him "a total failure", and the bishop had said, "You must go elsewhere." The cardinal prefect had written, "Just go at once."

As the train sped on, Father Tolton recalled his first trip to Chicago en route to Rome. He remembered the joy and exuberance of that journey, and as he began to compare it with the train ride he was taking now, bitter thoughts forced themselves into his mind. He drove them away as best he could and began to recite his Office.

19

CHICAGO'S FIRST BLACK PARISH

Saint Mary's Church, at Ninth and Wabash Streets, became the cradle of organized black Catholicism in Chicago and a landmark in its ecclesiastical history. The church, built in 1835, had been purchased from the Congregationalists by Bishop Thomas Foley, as an emergency measure when Holy Name Cathedral was destroyed in the 1871 Chicago Fire.

The pastor of Saint Mary's Church, Father Joseph Rowles, was the first priest of the city to inaugurate an apostolate to the blacks of Chicago and to give encouragement to their leaders, who were working to establish a place for communal worship. Father Rowles enlisted the help of his assistants, Father A. P. Lonergan and Father John McMullen, who were equally zealous and willing to help wherever they could.

In 1881, with permission from the bishop, these three priests invited blacks to a meeting to form an association, later to be known as Saint Augustine's Society. The members prayed together, listened to a religious instruction given by one of the fathers, and recruited new members. The common fund, to which all contributed and which was supplemented by donations from white friends, enabled the society to help the poor, visit the sick, and bury the dead among their people.

The steadfast good example of the members, their faithful attendance at prayer meetings, and their obvious faith were deciding factors when Bishop Foley, in response to a request from Father Rowles, gave permission for the celebration of Mass in the ground floor area of Saint Mary's Church. The official establishment of Chicago's first black parish took place in 1882, when Father McMullen offered Mass for the first time in this setting. Because the congregation grew out of the Saint Augustine Society, the basement place of worship came to be designated as Saint Augustine's Church. Black Catholics attended Mass there for seven years.

The membership of Saint Augustine's was made up of persons from parishes where blacks were barred, newcomers from the South, and sometimes blacks of other denominations who were attracted by the charity and self-sacrifice of priests and parishioners. The subparish, however, was unstable, the membership transitory, and the whole project almost entirely dependent upon Saint Mary's parish for material support. The common fund, set up earlier, was not adequate to pay for all parish expenses because the Saint Augustine Society drew heavily from it in order to carry on their corporal works of mercy. The strength of the congregation lay in the dedicated service of the pioneer members toward their less "advantaged" neighbors and in their unshakable faith. Also, they wanted a pastor of their own, and they were eager to have a priest of their own race.

In the year 1887 a delegation from the parish requested the incumbent archbishop, Patrick Feehan, to appoint Father Tolton as their spiritual leader. The archbishop, who knew about the black priest's unfortunate experience in Quincy, made immediate efforts to fulfill the request. Much correspondence and much waiting were required to effect the transfer of Father Tolton from the diocese of Alton to the archdiocese of Chicago. Finally Archbishop Feehan received word that Father Tolton was free to come.

In order to avoid publicity and an exuberant welcome, Father Tolton decided not to announce the exact date of his coming. While still in Quincy he had asked a friend, a black workman formerly from Quincy, to secure a lodging place for him in a "Negro district" of Chicago. When Father Tolton arrived in the city, a week before Christmas of 1889, he went directly to the apartment building at 2251 South Indiana Avenue. He found the room that his friend had rented for him. Even though the place was dark and dingy, Father Tolton experienced a sense of safety. He was among his own. Then too, he knew that he had forestalled embarrassment for himself and others in the matter of finding a place for him, a Negro, to live.

Father Tolton's first meeting with his new ecclesiastical superior was satisfying and heartening. Archbishop Feehan immediately appointed him pastor of "Saint Augustine's Church" and intimated that in time the blacks would be able to move out of Saint Mary's Church, and, in fact, he already had the promise of a large donation toward a new church. The archbishop then told Father Tolton that he had full jurisdiction of all the blacks in Chicago and that he had the authority to exercise all his priestly powers in their behalf. Father Tolton, not realizing the magnitude of the commission, smiled broadly. Later, in a letter to a Josephite priest, dated January 25, 1890, he said of the archbishop, "He is an elegant bishop. I love him."

Because Father Tolton had arrived in Chicago only a few days earlier, the people of "Saint Augustine's Church" did not know they had a pastor of their own until they came for the ten o'clock Mass. It was Father Tolton's first Sunday in

the city. Accompanied by Father Rowles, he walked down
the stone steps to the basement. There he met his congregation for the first time—a knot of worshipers, fewer than
thirty persons huddled shyly in a corner before the makeshift
altar.

Father Tolton noticed at once that the place lacked the
ordinary church atmosphere. It was a parish hall used alter-
nately as a meeting center and a place of divine worship. Ordinarily the Blessed Sacrament was not present. For that reason the new pastor was not too surprised when the people
talked out loud, came forward immediately to greet him,
grasped his hands, and continued to speak words of welcome. Some stood in awe as they noticed his red sash, unaware that it signified his association with the papal college;
others knelt at his feet and murmured words of gladness or
wept for sheer joy because they had a pastor, "one of their
own".

Father Tolton wiped his eyes and found his voice; he
spoke to the group in soft trembling accents. He thanked
them for their warm welcome and told them that he was
very happy to be their pastor.

Then, with Father Rowles at his side, Father Tolton offered Mass in Chicago's first black church. After the service
a repetition of hearty handshaking took place on the street
outside the church. Many white people coming out at the
same hour also grasped the black hand and expressed their
good wishes.

From the very outset Father Tolton enjoyed the hospitality of Father Rowles in the rectory of Saint Mary's parish.
He was introduced to the members of the Saint Augustine
Society and soon became acquainted with its history and its
purpose. The parish records handed over by Father Rowles
showed large figures of indebtedness as well as encouraging

assets. "The Saint Augustine Society has done well", Father Rowles informed him. "It has raised considerable sums by holding fairs, picnics, and social projects in their own neighborhoods. You can depend upon them, Father, to pay your salary and also help you with other expenses."

Back in his one-room apartment in the black ghetto, Father Tolton began to organize his effects, his duties, and his thoughts. The warm reception he had received from his people at the church inspired him. Plans for the future rose up in his mind—plans which, in his excited state, reached gigantic proportions. Then one by one he saw the problems confronting him in his new assignment. He thought wistfully of Saint Joseph's Church in Quincy; how beautiful and fitting it was compared to the poorly furnished Saint Augustine's Church! But then, Archbishop Feehan had said there would be a new church for the blacks.

Father Tolton could not easily forget his unfortunate experiences in Quincy. He must have failed his parishioners there, he thought, because many of them left the church; he must have disappointed his white friends, for they deserted him when difficulties loomed. He must have failed Father Weiss, his dean, who found it necessary to report him to the bishop. He failed the bishop too, because it was he who advised him to go elsewhere. Did he perhaps also fail the Sacred Congregation *de Propaganda Fide*?

In addition to these painful reminiscences, Father Tolton had proof that his "lack of success" had been noised abroad; his conjecture that this was a means of self-justification on the part of those who had exiled him did not lessen his anguish.

Another problem, one which harassed him day after day, concerned his own family. He had promised his mother when he left Quincy that he would bring her and his sister to Chicago as soon as he was settled. His present quarters were inadequate; it was a poor place, what we would call today a "cold-water" flat. He could not ask the diocese or his impoverished "parish" to find a home for his relatives. But he knew how desperately his mother wanted to leave Quincy and join him in Chicago.

Father Tolton was concerned and even torn by the letters of request that came to him from various prominent churchmen. He was asked to give addresses before various audiences and mainly in the churches of large cities in order to further the black apostolate. The Second Plenary Council of Baltimore, whose decrees demanded the Christianization and education of American blacks, had convened nearly a quarter century earlier. In their recommendation *De Nigrorum Salute Procuranda* they wrote, "We entreat priests that they devote to this work their labors, their time, and if it can be done, their whole life. Let superiors of religious houses select some of their members to come to the aid of the bishops; let secular priests whom God has called to his work offer themselves wholly." Consequently, some members of the hierarchy turned to Father Tolton as one who could help them do something about fulfilling the Council's decree in this neglected and difficult mission. Father Tolton's reaction is seen in his letter to Father John Slattery, S.S.J.

2251 Indiana Avenue
Chicago, Illinois
January 25, 1890

My dearest friend, Father Slattery:

Your kind letter has just been received and the contents read thoughtfully. I must say that at this moment I wish there were 27 Father Toltons, or colored priests at any rate, who could supply the demands. There are 27 letters here before me all asking me to come and lecture; come and give my kind assistance; all of them speaking in the same way. . . .

Your and Father McDermitt's letter are of some weight I must confess. Now, Father Slattery, what a grand thing it would be if I were a Josephite belonging to your rank of missionaries. I could then get over America and accomplish something. . . .

Therefore since I am a new hand here in this diocese, I don't think it would be very wise of me going off now to the different places that have called me. I have been here only four weeks. If you write to the archbishop, I don't care; if he says, go, I will go. But I think he does not want me to slight the people here. Therefore let everyone write to him and not to me and I will obey him.

Father Tolton's major problem, however, was the building of a church. Both the archbishop and Father Rowles had hinted repeatedly that the Saint Mary's parishioners needed the basement area for their own purposes. The problem became acute as the number of black Catholics began to increase. The time came when Father Tolton did not know which way to turn, and the fact of the matter was that his bishop did not have an immediate solution either.

The continued pressures from the white parishioners as well as from the clergy, toward having the blacks find a different place for worship, prompted Father Tolton to seek advice from Archbishop Feehan. The Negro priest suggested the opening of a store front church—a temporary chapel —in the heart of the black district. The archbishop readily gave his permission for such a chapel to be opened in the twenty-two-hundred block of South Indiana Avenue, next door to Father Tolton's rooming house. This arrangement, made in 1891, was more satisfactory even though the chapel was located in a rundown section of the city. Blacks who did not attend the so-called Saint Augustine's Church, mainly because it was too far away, came in greater numbers to "Saint Monica's Chapel", as the store front church was to be called.

That same year the nineteen black converts from the former Saint Joseph's parish in Quincy, whom Father Tolton mentioned in his letter to the prefect of the Sacred Congregation, joined him in his Chicago parish. The Saint Augustine Society found a rectory for Father Tolton—a house located at 448–36th Street. Now he could bring his mother and his sister to Chicago.

Anne Tolton, Father Tolton's sister

Father Tolton was heartened by the hundred or more regular communicants who now made up his parish. More than ever he wanted them to have a church of their own. Together with his people the priest planned a magnificent church—a church for their children's children. Supported by the indomitable faith of Father Tolton and his mother, who knew the goodness of the Lord, the people worked to make this dream come true.

20

SAINT MONICA'S CHURCH IN CHICAGO

It was understood from the outset that Saint Monica's Chapel on South Indiana Avenue was an emergency measure. Archbishop Feehan, who had sanctioned the opening of a store front church, knew that it was merely temporary, that it would soon be too small for the growing black parish, and, above all, that it was not a proper setting for divine worship. Therefore, he told Father Tolton to begin at once with plans for a church. The archbishop bought a lot in the northeast corner of 35th and Dearborn Streets to be used for this purpose. Funds for the purchase were made available because of the so-called O'Neill donation, of which Archbishop Feehan had spoken during the first meeting with Father Tolton.

As early as 1888, Mrs. Anne O'Neill donated $10,000 toward a black church. She and other Catholic leaders believed that the spiritual life of the race would be improved, their determination aroused, and their faith strengthened if they were given the opportunity to do their part in building and supporting a parish.

The magnitude of the task assigned to Father Tolton can be understood only in the light of his times and in a study of the economic and social status of Chicago's blacks.

A survey of this period made by Estelle Scott in "Growth

of the Negro Community,"[1] states that the black population of Chicago was 27,000. Most of them lived in a segregated section that began at the edge of the downtown
business district and ran to 35th Street between State and
Wentworth. Many of them worked as personal servants in
private homes of almost any part of the city. Hotels and
restaurants also employed many of them for wages rang-
ing from five to thirty dollars a week. Only about fifty
to seventy-five workers held positions in municipal, state,
and government departments. These received salaries rang-
ing from seventy-five to 125 dollars per month. The bulk of
the black population was made up of dependents—women,
children, aged, and sick. No small part was jobless, transient,
shiftless, or alienated. This settlement of the late nineteenth
century was far from having a solid or unified society.

The *Conservator*, a black newspaper, states that the rapidly
growing population, by community consensus, actually fell
into three broad social groups. One class, known as "re-
spectables", were poor or moderately prosperous; they were
regular churchgoers, though often unrestrained in their worship and uninhibited in their ordinary behavior. A second
group, who called themselves "refined" because of their education and social status, looked down upon the "respecta-
bles" because they could not sanction their less decorous
actions and lack of social amenities. These two classes, however, had one thing in common. They were critical of the
third class—the "riffraff" or sinners, who were not church
members, ignorant, very undisciplined, and, therefore, a dis-
grace to the whole black community. The "refined" people
thought of themselves as defenders of the race; they were

---

[1] University of Chicago, W.P.A. Project 3684.

often embarrassed by their less cultured fellowmen. They felt that these should be forced into right conduct with ridicule, sarcasm, education, and, as a last resort, "law".

Saint Monica's Church in Chicago

The site selected for Saint Monica's Church, as it was to be called later, lay in a poor neighborhood, one that was becoming progressively more undesirable. It was in one of the city's blighted or slum areas and contingent to the "vice district". The place was surrounded by neglected tenement houses and small shacks, buildings with boarded windows, dirty alleys, and littered streets.

This combination of adverse factors explains the Herculean task facing Father Tolton as he attempted to organize a parish and began to collect the funds needed for the construction of a church. Except for the vacant lot on 35th and Dearborn Streets, purchased with the O'Neill donation, Father Tolton and his loyal friends had nothing.

A letter, dated January 25, 1890, which Father Tolton wrote to his Josephite friend Father Slattery, reflects his attitude toward the project:

Here I am hard at work. . . . We have secured a site on which
to build a church as soon as we have the means to begin. So
you see I am rushed now and have a lot on my mind. . . .

I had to refuse going to some places to give addresses as I
had too much to do going around getting the names of my
people and organizing a parish. These poor people have been
left in a bag with both ends open if I may say it that way.

As soon as the project of building a church was officially launched, Father Tolton inspired his small congregation with his own deep faith and contagious zeal. Saint
Augustine's Society, upon which the pastor relied for moral
and material support, raised a considerable sum and called
it their "church fund". This was separate from their regular
fund—the money they raised and needed to carry on their
work of mercy among the needy. Father Tolton realized that
he could not count very much on his parishioners for the finances necessary in the building of a church. With the sanction of Archbishop Feehan he appointed Lincoln C. Valle,
a black parishioner and one of his trustees, to solicit funds
from people in other parts of the city. In a letter dated August 7, 1899, Mr. Valle informed the Josephite Father Slattery that he had worked with Father Tolton for four years
and that he had collected much of the money for the church
from the white people of Chicago.

The annual dividend of the so-called Negro and Indian
Fund, though small, proved helpful for the struggling parish.
This source of financial assistance was made possible through
the efforts of American bishops when they convened in 1884
for the Third Plenary Council. On that occasion it was decreed that a special collection for Indians and blacks be taken
up in every diocese of the whole country.

While attending a Catholic Colored Congress in Washington D.C. in 1889, Father Tolton met a Josephite priest, Father Alfred B. Leeson, and other delegates interested in financing black missions. At this time, too, Father Tolton first learned about Katherine Drexel, foundress of the Sisters of the Blessed Sacrament in Philadelphia.

Katherine Drexel, daughter of Francis Drexel, Jr., head of the world-famous banking house of Drexel and Company, and Father Tolton shared a common interest and concern: the welfare of the blacks.

Upon the death of their father in 1885, Katherine and her two sisters became the heiresses of an immense fortune. The education and religious training Katherine received led her to see the racial injustice inflicted upon some minority groups. She was especially impressed by the appeal of the bishops at the Third Plenary Council for Indian and Negro missions. In a private audience of Pope Leo XIII in January 1887, Katherine mentioned this interest and her willingness to use her fortune in that cause. At that time the Pontiff asked, "Why not become a missionary yourself, my child?" This question settled the girl's vocation for life. With thirteen other young women she founded the community of the Sisters of the Blessed Sacrament, dedicated to the welfare of Indians and Negroes.

Mother Drexel's community and its purpose were publicized as early as 1890, a year before its canonical establishment. Consequently, Father Tolton's appeals to her for financial assistance in his pioneer work in Chicago coincide with the formative period of this religious congregation; it accounts for the fact that the initial requests did not always receive an immediate response.

Although the priest's letters to Mother Katherine do not reveal the amounts she sent, the records at the Cornwells

Heights motherhouse of the community indicate that the annual payments made to the Negro mission in Chicago during the lifetime of Father Tolton amounted to $36,000.

On September 30, 1890, in the first of three letters to Mother Katherine preserved in the community's archives, Father Tolton wrote:

Sister Katherine
Dear Madam:

I wrote a letter to you once before but found out later on that I had misdirected it, sending it to Philadelphia instead of to Pittsburgh.

I heard from all of the colored delegates (at the convention) that you kindly consented to give a helping hand to the colored missions. This was the spirit of my first letter, namely to ask you for your kind assistance.

I am in a new missionary field and have nothing to start with. I hope you will assist us if it is not asking too much of you; but I suppose that all of your charity is nearly exhausted by this time as you have helped so many missions. I hope that you will get the other letter I sent. I misdirected it, being misinformed as to your place.

A. Tolton (a colored priest)

Naturally Father Tolton was disappointed in not receiving the kind of help that he had heard of other missions receiving. Yet he waited for almost a year before he made another appeal. By this time the need for funds had become acute, and he feared that the whole project would have to be postponed unless money was made available to pay for the materials and to hire laborers. In the face of this difficulty the priest wrote again on May 12, 1891:

My dear Mother Katherine:

I am quite sure that you are bothered considerably now attending to your own work and arranging matters for your new order, which I am sure will be a blessing for our entire race. Father Leeson asked me last week if I had written you a letter. I told him that I did, and he said, "Write again; perhaps Sister has forgotten you." I told him that I did not think you would forget us, only I did not desire to be too hasty. We are glad we can look forward in hope. Here in Chicago we have so many promises, but that will not help us. Still I must confess that I have done real well being here only one and a half years. I have in all 260 souls to render an account for before God's majesty. There really are 600 in all, but they have become like unto dead branches of a tree and without moisture because no one has taken care of them.

Just last Sunday night I was called to the deathbed of a colored woman who had been away from her duties for nine years because she was hurled out of a white church and even cursed by the Irish member. Very bad indeed! She sent for me and thanked God that she had a priest to send for.

These dear people feel proud that they have a priest to look after them. Even Protestants, when sick, will send for me in preference to their preachers, and they treat me with the greatest respect. Not one is prejudiced at all. That makes me feel that there is a great work for me here.

Sister, please answer if you have time enough to do so as I would very much like to hear from you.

Rev. A. Tolton

Less than a month later Father Tolton wrote to Mother Katherine again. His letter, dated June 3, 1891, is an apology rather than an appeal.

Dear Mother Katherine:

I deem it necessary to write you this letter to ask that you please forgive me for vexing you so far. One priest, of course, wrote to me stating that all of us fathers on the colored missions are almost setting you crazy, that you have too many requests to tend to. I am sorry that I vexed you. Of course, I expected such a letter from someone, so I will apologize at once, I for one cannot tell how to conduct myself when I see one person at last showing love for the colored race.

One thing I do know, and that is that it took the Catholic Church one hundred years here in America to show up such a person as yourself. That is the reason why you have so much bother now and so many extending their hands to you to get a lift.

In the whole history of the Church in America we can't find another person who has sworn to lay out a treasury for the sole benefit of the colored and the Indians. As I stand alone as the first Negro priest of America, so you, Mother Katherine, stand alone as the first one to make such a sacrifice for the cause of the downtrodden race. Therefore, the South is looking on with angry eyes; the North in many places is criticizing every act, just as it is watching over every move I make. I suppose that is the reason we had no Negro priest before this day. They watch us the same as the Pharisees did our Lord. They watched him all the time. I really feel that there will be a great stir all over the United States when I begin my church. I shall work and pull at it as long as God gives me life, for I see that I have powers and principalities to resist anywhere and everywhere I go.

The world is indeed a great book, and I have read many of its pages. So this letter is to ask that you excuse me if I have bothered you too much. I know that you have a lot to do, for I am sure that you have letters from all sides of America and even outside of it.

Indian missionaries have always been writing to me for aid, but I couldn't render them anything. I was in extreme need myself; but if I had anything to send I would send it right off, but God has destined it this way, and I must be contented.

Now, Sister, just when you get rested and are ready to send, all well and good. I will stop vexing your mind by my letters.

Respectfully,
A. Tolton

Late in 1891, when the building fund had increased sufficiently, Archbishop Feehan granted permission to begin the actual construction of the church. "A Negro architect, Negro contractors, and workmen put up the building," writes Father A. Zimmermann S.V.D., in his work *The Beginning of an Era*, "and white Catholics donated liberally."

Archbishop Feehan laid the cornerstone for the church and dedicated it to Saint Monica. Mrs. Caecilia Hubbard Barnett, who was present for the dedicatory ceremony, still has this recollection: "It was a big day for the parish and for the whole neighborhood. Archbishop Feehan and many priests were present. It was said that many valuable articles were put into the cornerstone."

An item among the papers of Father Tolton, apparently a journal entry, states, "A Roman Catholic archbishop in his robes at the cornerstone laying saw a little child in the crowd. He took it up in his arms and kissed it before a multitude of three thousand persons. Real spirit of Jesus Christ shown in the Catholic Church by this bishop."

Two years later, in 1893, when Saint Monica's Church was only about half completed, construction was halted for lack of funds. A temporary roof was put on, and services were begun. "The structure was planned with the idea of expansion," wrote Mrs. Blanche Rodney, a pioneer member of the parish, "and therefore, because they did not have money, services were held when the church had only plain frosted windows, no baptistery, no confessionals (confessions were heard in the sacristy), and a flat roof instead of the contemplated gables and spires."

Father Zimmermann's record states, "The future looked very bright for Father Tolton and his little flock. About thirty persons had joined him as regular members of the Saint Mary's Church basement, and fifty more were added when the store front chapel was opened on Indiana Avenue. Now in Saint Monica's Church his congregation grew by leaps and bounds." Father Tolton himself informed Mother Katherine Drexel that he "was ministering to six hundred Negroes scattered about Chicago".

There were times when Father Tolton felt physically unable to carry on the burdens of his pastorate; he shrugged off the occasional spells of illness and lack of energy with the determination that his duties came first. He lived in a house behind the church, his mother keeping up the place for him and ministering to his personal needs. "Mother Tolton", as she was affectionately called by the parishioners, was the sacristan, and with the help of some young girls, among them Caecilia Hubbard, later Mrs. Barnett, she kept the church spotless. Mrs. Tolton was also a member of the parish choir —one of the "faithful volunteers", as Mrs. Barnett called them. "A small hand-pumped organ was all we had," says Mrs. Barnett, "and the organist was paid twelve dollars a month."

According to Father Zimmermann's account, "Father Tolton had a charming personality. His voice when he sang the High Masses was beautiful. His culture was remarkable—

the Eternal City had left its mark on him. He dreamed and planned for the day when his people would finish the structure he had begun and have a building to which they could point with the greatest pride as their very own.

Father Tolton's concern, however, was not exclusively about the building and financing of the church. He was far more anxious about the spiritual welfare of his people, many of whom were still leading irregular and dissolute lives. In an effort to reclaim the erring and to lead more people to Christ, Father Tolton organized adult instruction classes. He engaged several lay persons to help teach the children on Sundays, and he himself taught Christian doctrine after both Masses on Sunday and before the afternoon Vespers.

There were times, however, when he was completely discouraged. He saw the futility of trying to give spiritual help to people who were desperately in need of material assistance. Funds collected for the completion of Saint Monica's Church had to be used for food, medicine, clothes, and adequate shelter. He was forced to make repeated appeals to the Saint Augustine Society in order to alleviate the sufferings of poverty-stricken families. Through his mediation, destitute families received help from the Catholic organization known as the Visitation and Aid Society. In a letter to Father Slattery preserved in the Josephite archives, Miss Mary C. Elmore, a Franciscan tertiary and board member of the Visitation and Aid Society, writes the following:

> I attended 10:00 o'clock Mass yesterday with Father Tolton's congregation, and I had the opportunity of speaking with my good friend, the Negro priest. I thought he was going to attend the Congress, but he said he was feeling so ill that he was afraid he would not be able to undertake the journey. Poor Father—it seems strange that after all the gush about

the "dear Negro", he is left to struggle alone in poverty and humility, grappling with the giant task of founding a church and congregation in Chicago. We who come in contact with him in our labors and are witnesses of his ardent charity and self-denying zeal feel ourselves privileged to bow the knee for his saintly blessing.

Father Tolton learned about another source from which to procure food and clothing for the destitute and hospitalization for the sick and dying, namely, the Ladies Catholic Benevolent Association. This national association had been founded in Erie, Pennsylvania, only in 1890. With the encouragement of Father Tolton, Saint Monica's branch of the L.C.B.A. was established under the leadership of Mrs. Susie Wilson. It has the distinction of being the first in the state of Illinois and the only Negro unit in the United States. This branch took its name from Saint Monica's Church and even today retains its title and purpose and is active in Chicago.

From the letter of Mary C. Elmore we gain the first intimation that Father Tolton was battling with ill health. His parishioners knew that he was wearing himself out by hard work and privation. They had begun to notice his increasing weakness and lack of endurance. On several occasions during the past year Father Tolton had asked the Mass server to bring a chair because he could not stand and deliver the sermon. At other times he shortened or even omitted his homily because his voice failed or because a nagging cough interfered. Mrs. Susie Wilson, a prominent woman of the parish, said she often saw beads of perspiration on the priest's brow when he celebrated Mass or distributed Holy Communion, and even during the cool seasons. "He overtaxed himself while helping others", states the Chicago *Defender* of July 12, 1945. "In his position at Saint Monica's Church he was so conscientious and diligent when he labored for the Church, congregation, and community, that his health began to fail."

In spite of his fatigue, Father Tolton made the daily rounds in his parish, stepping over the uneven brick pavements and cobbled sidewalks or climbing steep rickety stairs. All too often he was horrified by the squalor, the ravages of poverty and disease, the prevalence of dissipation and vice. Many of his people were ex-slaves and totally illiterate; others suffered just as severely from moral deprivation.

The black-robed priest became a familiar figure in the littered streets and foul-smelling alleys of his district. He laid aside his red sash—the emblem of his affiliation with the pontifical seminary—and appeared always in his well-worn, faded cassock. Day after day he was seen coming in or out of the shacks, the rat-infested hovels and tenement houses. He listened compassionately to complaints of unemployment, desertion, injustice, depravity. Father Tolton knew how to bring hope and comfort to the sick and dying; he knew how to mitigate human suffering and sorrow because he himself had experienced the lash of the slave driver as well as the lash of the white man's tongue. His great heart ached for all his fellow blacks, not just for the members of his parish. It is safe to say that Father Tolton understood the soul of his race better than did any other cleric or prelate of his time.

Father Tolton won the admiration of people and priests alike. There were those who knew him to be a highly gifted man, a priest stamped with the culture and education of the pontifical college in Rome, a beautiful singer, and an eloquent speaker. And yet he was tireless and cheerful in his day after day, year after year, ministry to the unschooled, the downtrodden, and the poverty-stricken members of his parish.

Father Tolton's round of duties did not give him time

to fraternize with the clergy of Chicago as he had done in Quincy, although he was warmly received by all and invited to their rectories. In Chicago too, he became known as "Good Father Gus" when he met white priests on special occasions or when he joined them at the annual priests' retreat.

The sole relaxation and pleasure that Father Tolton allowed himself was his far-into-the-night playing on the accordion. He relived all his seminary years as he sang song after song to his own accompaniment.

The late Monsignor Theodore Warning, of the archdiocese of Dubuque, often spoke of an experience he had during a summer session at the University of Chicago in 1896. Hoping to find a place to live near campus, he made inquiries at a small house near a South Side church. The black woman who responded to the knock bowed graciously as she asked him to come inside. Monsignor asked to see the pastor. "The pastor," she said, smiling, "he is my son." Monsignor Warning called his six-week stay as guest of Father Tolton and his mother "a sacred experience". It had obviously made a lasting impression, for it was more than a quarter century later when he added the following account:

> They lived in a poorly furnished but very clean house. The meals were simple affairs. Father Tolton, his mother, and I sat at a table having an oil cloth cover. A kerosene lamp stood in the middle. On the wall directly behind Father Tolton's place hung a large black rosary, most likely one he had brought from Rome. As soon as the evening meal was over Father Tolton would rise and take the beads from the nail. He kissed the large crucifix reverently. We all knelt on the bare floor while the Negro priest, in a low voice, led the prayers with deliberate slowness and with unmistakable fervor.

"The Catholic Church is the Church for our people", Father Tolton used to say in his addresses to large-city audiences, which he gave before he came to Chicago. Now, however, there were times when his own faith in this assertion was badly shaken. He wondered why his work as a spiritual leader made such slow progress, why after all these years of unstinting labor—organizing a parish and trying to build a church—he had only a half finished structure and could count very few other tangible achievements. Some of the other priests were quick to say that this was no reflection on him, and they assured Father Tolton that his exemplary zeal and his faithful priestly life would eventually bring the results he desired.

Men of the parish who helped Father Tolton in special ways were Mr. William Hubbard and Mr. Peter Adler, both of whom donated their services as sexton, usher, secretary, and general assistant. Mr. Lincoln Valle also worked without remuneration while he continued to solicit funds. Other members of the parish referred to these three men as "Father Tolton's Bodyguard" and understood it as a position of honor.

Even the low, roofless Saint Monica's Church, whose dark gray stone walls were capped by a temporary cover of black tiling, was far from being debt-free. The staggering bills which lay on the priest's desk had to be paid before construction could be continued. Mr. Valle had to admit that collections were falling off. "People promise to pay", he told Father Tolton, "if and when the church is finished." And Father Tolton had to admit that the first enthusiasm of his parishioners had reached a low ebb because the building process had come to a standstill.

Of the nine hundred black Catholics mentioned by Archbishop Feehan in his first meeting with Father Tolton, some six hundred had registered at Saint Monica's Church. Many of these came from distant parts of the city. In time these blacks came to realize that they were not barred from attending the churches nearer their homes. Consequently there was a considerable decrease in the number of worshipers at Saint Monica's Church. Then, on the other hand, because the black church was conveniently located for some members of neighboring white parishes—Saint George on 39th Street near Wentworth, Saint James at 29th and Wabash, and Saint Elizabeth at 41st and Wabash—these often chose to attend Mass at Saint Monica's Church. "The intermingling of races in the churches", writes Caecilia Hubbard Barnett, "did begin to stir up feelings of segregation and prejudice. This hurt Father Tolton keenly because after six years in Rome he had not completely realized the difference between white and black."

Neither Father Tolton nor his people objected to the presence of white people in their church, especially since there was ample room. However, the pastor was disturbed by the attitude of those priests and people who, unconcerned about the distance blacks had to travel, thought they should all attend Saint Monica's Church.

Father Tolton was sincerely proud of his color and totally dedicated to the welfare and success of his race. Any indignity inflicted upon his people was absolutely a personal offense. Painfully aware of his experiences in Quincy, Father Tolton now tended to avoid any clash with other pastors and their parishioners. A time had come, it seemed to him, for the reopening of old wounds—a new realization of that fear of "what he may experience from the dominant race in America", as stated in the recommendation by the cardinal prefect.

"He felt unwanted by other priests," wrote Mrs. Barnett, "so he stayed by himself and played his accordion and read his many books. He was a scholar. Besides English, he spoke Italian, German, and French."

But for Father Tolton there were no lonely hours in the rectory, because his devoted mother, whom he cherished above all others, was always there to help, comfort, and encourage. The priest's reverence for her and Mrs. Tolton's concern for him and the church so edified the parishioners that they always referred to her as Mother, or Mother Tolton.

Father Tolton was heartened by the knowledge that he had won the esteem and affection of his people. They thought of him as their own priest and honored him as a good kind father. Father Tolton's sermons, admonitions, and instructions, always theologically sound, were geared to the intellectual level of his flock.

Hours of anguish and discouragement now became a part of Father Tolton's life. While performing his round of duties he suffered more and more from fatigue and exhaustion. But he would not give up because he felt the church building had to be completed. Father Tolton looked wistfully at other churches of the city. Magnificent edifices with immense spires, even twin spires, and lofty towers with chimes and bells sprang up around his slum parish, dwarfing Saint Monica's, the unfinished, flat-roofed church—the black center of worship. The sight of those edifices—tokens of white people's faith—awakened a longing which threatened to drown his courage. He lamented the fact that he and his people had only this humble abode for the King of Kings.

However, as Father Tolton knelt before the altar in the bare church, comfort and consolation came to him from the Divine Presence. He knew that God understood him, guided and directed him; he did not know that the imposing churches with spires and bells actually were the "Negro churches" of the future.

21

HIS LIFE FOR HIS FRIENDS

Father Tolton is dead.

This news, announced in Chicago's papers on July 10, 1897, plunged the black community into a state of shock. The word flew from mouth to mouth. Groups of startled people gathered outside of shacks and tenements and on street corners. Their voices gave vent to grief. Women fell sobbing into each other's arms; children halted in their play and stood about in wide-eyed wonder. Men dashed tears from their eyes. As the sorrow and excitement mounted, people began to ask incessantly questions that seemed to have no answer.

"What happened?" "Was he sick?" "Was he hurt?" "Was he slugged?" "Does Mother Tolton know?"

Despite the 105-degree heat wave that gripped the whole city, Father Tolton's bereaved people walked aimlessly under the burning sun. Parishioners went in and out of Saint Monica's Church seeking comfort, weeping, and praying. Small groups met on the church steps and spoke in hushed broken whispers.

"What will we do without Father Tolton?" "What will become of our church?" "Who will look after us now?"

Some of the people recalled Father Tolton's announcement of the previous Sunday. He had told the congregation that he would be away from the parish for several days

and that he would return on Friday; that confessions would
be heard on Saturday afternoon and evening as usual; that
a priest from Saint Elizabeth's Church had agreed to take
care of emergency sick calls. As a final announcement Father
Tolton, in his confiding way, explained to his people that
he was going to make the annual spiritual retreat which was
being conducted at Saint Viator's College in Bourbonnais
for the priests of the archdiocese of Chicago.

"I will never forget that Sunday of July 4, 1897", said
Mrs. Elsie Shepherd, a pioneer member of the parish. "Father Tolton told us all about the nature of a retreat. He said
it was a three-day vacation from ordinary duties in order to
give a person the chance to think more seriously of his own
spiritual progress; that it was a time to converse with God
and to gain new strength and energy to carry on the duties
of one's vocation."

There was no doubt a general feeling of satisfaction at
the announcement that Father Tolton would have this short
respite from his arduous duties. Now, in the hour of their
great grief they admitted they had been relieved, even happy,
that their beloved pastor would have a "vacation", as he had
called it. One after another tear-choked voice recalled symp-
toms of Father Tolton's ill health: how he often wiped his
brow while at the altar, how his hand shook when he distributed Holy Communion, how slowly he walked, and the
many times he had to sit down while he preached.

New pangs of grief and bereavement gripped his people
as details of the tragedy appeared in Chicago's newspapers:

Father Tolton was on his way home from Bourbonnais, about
one hundred miles away, where he had attended a three-day
priests' retreat. He stepped off the train at the 35th station
near the lake and began walking toward his rectory located
at 448–36th Street. It was shortly before noon, and the tem-

perature had reached 105 degrees. Father Tolton seemed to grow weak; he swayed back and forth and then fell heavily to the sidewalk. From all sides people rushed to his assistance. They moved him to a cooler spot. The Stanton Avenue police patrol took him to the hospital.

The Sisters of Mercy, who conducted Mercy Hospital at 2537 Prairie Avenue, aided the stricken priest. Doctors and nurses were in constant attendance. The hospital chaplain remained at the bedside. He administered the sacrament of the last anointing and recited the prayers for the dying. Father Tolton did not regain consciousness, and as the afternoon wore on his fever mounted and his breathing became increasingly laborious. He died that evening, while his mother and sister, the chaplain, and several Sisters of Mercy knelt in prayer.

According to the hospital records Father Augustine Tolton died of heat stroke and uremia on July 9, 1897, at the age of forty-three.

All day Sunday the remains of Father Tolton lay in state at Saint Monica's Church. A chalice and a stole—symbols of the priesthood—stood on the casket. The high esteem that the black priest had won was evidenced by the thousands of people from all over the city who filed through the church to pay their respects. In the evening of that day priests filled the church to recite the Office of the Dead.

Father John Gilliam, vicar general of the archdiocese, was delegated by Archbishop Feehan to offer the solemn Requiem Mass for Father Tolton on Monday, July 12, 1897. More than one hundred white priests crowded in the sanctuary and front pews of Saint Monica's Church. Father T. Mooney, chancellor of the archdiocese, gave the sermon.

According to the Chicago *Daily News* for July 12, 1897,

the crowd was so great in Saint Monica's Church at the funeral services of Father Tolton that all the seats were filled long before the 10:00 Mass, and the line extended out into the street. Children were not allowed to view the remains which lay in state near the front of the church; slender white candles surrounded the casket and gave a blaze of light. The people walked down one aisle, viewed the remains of their beloved pastor, and went back another aisle out into the street. . . .

Expecting a crowd, Father Daniel Riordan, pastor of Saint Elizabeth's Church, who was responsible for funeral arrangements, had asked for a detail of police to help handle the multitude, and his appeal was answered by Sergeant Farrel who sent ten of the finest-looking officers in the station.

Because it was impossible for most of the people to enter the church, many of them remained outside and formed a circle around the building. Even these heard the funeral sermon. Father Mooney reviewed the departed pastor's heroic deeds and tireless efforts; he spoke words of comfort to the sorrowing parishioners and exhorted them to continue on the way Father Tolton had charted; above all, he encouraged them to fulfill the deceased priest's most cherished hope—to complete Saint Monica's Church.

After the Mass some of the blacks gathered around the rectory to comfort the priest's heartbroken mother and sister; others stood around in small groups near the church and in awed whispers discussed the fate that had befallen their beloved pastor.

During his lifetime Father Tolton had often expressed the desire to be interred in the priests' lot of Saint Peter's cemetery in Quincy. He wanted to be buried there and also to have a funeral Mass at Saint Peter's Church—the church of his childhood, his First Communion, and his confirmation. In deference to his wish, preparations were made to take the body to Quincy. Meanwhile it continued to lie in state at Saint Monica's Church until late evening. For the greater part of that day both blacks and whites gathered in small groups and stood in mute sorrow and prayerful attitudes. Members of the grieving parish kept a constant vigil beside the casket until the remains were taken to the railroad station by a horse-drawn hearse.

On the journey back to Quincy, Father Tolton's body was accompanied by Father J. Brecks, friend and spiritual director of the deceased, and representing the Chicago clergy; by his mother and sister; by parish delegates James Bowles and Samuel Neals and several white and black members of Chicago's Catholic organizations.

The cortege arrived at Quincy on the morning of July 13. Twelve priests of Quincy, among them several Franciscan fathers, were at the station to meet the funeral party and to accompany the body of Father Tolton to Saint Peter's Church. Here, as at Saint Monica's, every place in the church was taken, and lines of people stood in the aisles, in the gallery, and outside. Through this crowd, motionless and hushed, pallbearers J. J. Flynn, Jerry Shea, Fred Schulteis, Patrick McGuire, J. B. Menke, and John Hellhake carried the casket into the church. Father Joseph Kerr, pastor of Saint Peter's Church (since the death of Father McGirr in 1893), offered the Requiem Mass.

Many people in the crowd, among whom there was a mere sprinkling of blacks, remembered Father Tolton when he was a factory worker; they remembered him as Mass server and parish custodian; others thought of him as a student, lay apostle, or friend; still others recalled the years of his priesthood at Saint Joseph's Church. They all came to pay their respects; they came to pray for his soul.

"There was seldom such a large funeral", states the Quincy

Journal of July 13, 1897. "The cortege was four blocks long, plus street cars which took the people as far as Dulden field. From there they walked to the cemetery."

Father Joseph Kerr gave the final benediction as the body of Father Tolton was laid to rest in the priests' lot.

Over the grave a modest marker was set which was later to be replaced by a large concrete cross. Today this monument bears the inscription:

Rev. Augustine Tolton
The First Colored Priest in the United States
Born in Brush Creek, Ralls County, Missouri, April 1, 1854
Ordained in Rome, Italy, April 24, 1886
Died July 9, 1897
Requiescat in Pace

Father Tolton's grave, Quincy

Their sad mission accomplished in the burial of Father Tolton, most of the mourners returned to their homes. The delegation from Chicago, however, lingered at the grave site until late afternoon, when the train was due to take them back to their own city.

The priests—diocesan and Franciscan—assembled at Saint Peter's Rectory. They were a quiet sobered group, each one preoccupied with his own unspoken reflections: "Why did Father Tolton want to be buried in Quincy?" "In a diocese and city from which he had been banished?" "What happened to the black parish in Quincy?" "Why was there no eulogy for Father Tolton after the Mass?"

There were answers for some of the questions: Saint Joseph's Church was closed when Father Tolton went to Chicago seven years earlier; when the small congregation scattered or moved to other cities, the school was also abandoned.

The priests in the rectory sat in silence or talked in subdued voices. They discussed the remarkable career of this priest, the obviously providential happenings in his life, and lamented his untimely death. Finally they agreed that Father Tolton had fulfilled his sacerdotal mission, that he had done this in a short time—fewer than twelve years.

Then the conversation centered on that morning's funeral Mass, with the huge crowd, Catholic and non-Catholic, whose eyes were riveted on the casket with the chalice and stole. Some of the priests admitted that they too had been moved by the celebrant's words which at that Requiem Mass became a tribute to the dead and sounded a warning for the living: "Pray brethren, that my sacrifice and yours may be acceptable to God the Father Almighty."

Finally the priests opened the subject of the black apostolate, its needs, its possibilities, and the impact of the work accomplished by the deceased leader, Father Tolton. Their scattered thoughts rested on the belief that Father Tolton understood the significance of his vocation; that he felt it was his mission to erase prejudice, distrust, and suspicion because these impeded the progress of his race; that his own life of holiness, courage, intelligence, and perseverance was unmistakable proof that a slave could become a good priest in the face of poverty and injustice.

Then the assembled priests realized and agreed that a eulogy would have been superfluous and in bad taste, because Father Augustine Tolton's whole life had been a sermon.

EPILOGUE:
THE SHEPHERDLESS FLOCK

The vacancy left by the death of Father Tolton brought Archbishop Feehan to reduce Saint Monica's parish to the status of a mission. He annexed it to Saint Elizabeth's Church, 41st Street and Wabash Avenue, and entrusted the people to Father Daniel Riordan. From then on, the only service held in Father Tolton's parish would be one Mass on Sunday, and there would be an opportunity for the sacrament of penance on Saturday.

It became more and more evident to observers that the passing of Father Tolton had dealt Saint Monica's parish an almost fatal blow. The black parishioners accepted the decision of the archbishop and the consequent efforts of Father Riordan and his assistants with either meager appreciation or downright defiance. Many of them resented the fact that their church services were reduced to the bare essentials.

The parish organizations that Father Tolton had established disbanded through lack of direction; adult instruction classes were discontinued, and convert making was not encouraged. The number of children who attended Sunday School dwindled to such an extent that the lay teachers dropped the classes.

When the more zealous members of Saint Monica's parish protested that their religious services were so meager, priests in charge pleaded, and justifiably so, lack of time and multiplicity of duties elsewhere. The blacks were especially offended by the insinuation that this mission church was an inconvenience.

These circumstances are recalled by Mrs. Blanche Rodney, onetime member of Saint Monica's parish. She states that mainly because their own church was unfinished, they watched the development and progress of Saint Elizabeth's parish with wistful eyes and ill-concealed envy. They noted the daily hours of divine worship, the flourishing school, the parish associations and activities—all of which were reminders of their own unfulfilled hopes and plans.

Some of the parish leaders and loyal friends of the church were thoroughly alarmed over the decrease in membership, general apathy, and growing religious indifference. Above all, they were distressed that the Catholic children who attended public schools accompanied their friends to Protestant churches. Black Catholics saw the need of more pastoral guidance and the urgent necessity of catechetical instruction. Children as well as adults learned only what they could understand from the Sunday scriptural readings and sermon.

Two years after the death of Father Tolton, members of Saint Monica's parish called a meeting to discuss the state of affairs and to formulate plans for action. First they decided upon a delegation to speak for them to the archbishop. From time to time reports had reached the black community that there were no priests available, and rumor had it that there was also a lack of willingness on the part of some priests to take the charge. In view of these conjectures members of the meeting suggested that they try to get a priest from the Josephite Society in Baltimore.

According to Mrs. Caecilia Hubbard Barnett, cited earlier, Mr. Lincoln Valle remembered, as Father Tolton's secretary, that the principal purpose of the Josephite Society is to work among black people and that Father Randolph Uncles, a black priest ordained in 1891, was a member of that society. This information immediately brought up the suggestion that a request be made to have Father Uncles take charge of Saint Monica's Church.

Mr. Valle was personally acquainted with Father John Slattery, superior of the Josephites; he had met this priest several times while he, with Father Tolton, had attended Catholic black congresses. Now, because he had the approval of the archbishop and the encouragement of Father Riordan, he felt free to make the request.

The letter written by Mr. Lincoln Valle, preserved in the Josephite archives, is reproduced here:

2713 State Street
Chicago, Illinois
August 7, 1899

Dear Father Slattery

The Colored Catholics, representative men in meeting assembled, have delegated me to say for them to you that they would like for you to give this church here for the colored people a priest from your order to take charge of the work here in Chicago.

Since the death of Father Tolton, the work has been at a standstill. The reason is that there has been no priest in absolute charge of the colored people. The Rev. Riordan of St. Elizabeth's Church has been in charge temporarily until some change could be made. It is now going on three years since this work has been on a standstill, after a hard struggle to get it where it is today; we can't stop right in the middle of the work.

I find that a great number of Catholic colored people here are in favor of Father Uncles if they are permitted to have him; not only because he is colored but because they feel that the classes of colored people outside of the faith in Chicago would take to a priest of their own race.

As far as the Catholics are concerned it makes no difference to them. I find myself that the intelligent northern Negro will without doubt follow their best men in the pulpit. If he is a White man he must be a man of wide experience among that class of Negroes. I single out the intelligent Negro, because when you interest him the others will follow.

I don't mean, Father, to dictate to you how you should make your selection. I simply mean to give you a little information of what I know is true, it being that I am thrown among these people for years.

The majority of the working force of this mission have set their heads together toward getting a pastor, and as I know more about the work here than they do, and also having an acquaintance with you, they have appointed me to write to you. They have also selected me to go with them to His Grace, the Archbishop, and lay the whole matter before him and in the meantime name the priest of their choice. This same body of men have called upon Rev. Riordan and told him of their intention, and he told the committee that he would be very glad if they would get a pastor because he did not have time to pay any more attention to the work and that he would gladly give up the books at once to the priest His Grace, the Archbishop might appoint. So you see, Father, the road is clear.

There is a good healthy sentiment here in Chicago among the Colored and the White people toward this work. I know of people here who would help us if we had a pastor and they won't do a thing until we get one. . . .

Again, the converts he [Father Tolton] got during the two missions given here are falling off on account of not having a priest minister to their wants and the few Colored Catholics we have coming to church are getting discouraged. The young children coming up around us, unless we take care of them in the church, they will seek the companionship of Protestants and lose their faith.

With these few facts, Father, I plead to you through these people to help us in reaching the ends spoken of. Personally I would like to see your Society out West. The world doesn't know enough about what you are doing for my people and I know there is no better field than in Chicago.

Please, Father, let me hear from you at your earliest convenience so I will know just what to submit to the Archbishop when he comes home from his trip.

Trusting that you will act favorable to us in this matter, I remain,

Your obedient servant,
Lincoln C. Valle

Weeks and months passed by without bringing Mr. Valle a reply from Father Slattery. The seeming disregard of the petition and the failure to get a resident pastor for Saint Monica's Church occasioned disillusionment and continued apathy among many black Catholics.

It was many months later when Mr. Valle learned that the members of Saint Joseph Society in Baltimore were facing grave problems of their own. For him it was an explanation of their silence regarding his request.

The storm and stress that had harassed the Society of Saint Joseph ever since it was established in America two decades earlier had entered upon its final and most crucial stage. The strained relations between the Baltimore community and the original foundation in Mill Hill, England, neared the breaking point. Matters dealing with finances, policies, and discipline became controversial and invited disruption. A lack of understanding on the part of the Mill Hill fathers of American customs and tradition led to the ultimate clash. Then internal factions among the fathers in America led eventually to the establishment in 1893 of a new group here. It became known as Saint Joseph's Society of the Sacred Heart, or simply the Josephite fathers. Those who wished to join the new society were released by Rome from their affiliation to the Mill Hill foundation; others returned to England; still others became diocesan priests. Five pioneers, among them Father Randolph Uncles, formed the American community with Father John Slattery as its founding superior.

It is conceivable that this state of affairs was not conducive toward further missionary commitments on the part of the community, and it affords a probable, but scarcely pardonable reason, for Father Slattery's failure even to acknowledge Mr. Valle's very reasonable letter.

When it became evident that the request for a Josephite pastor was not about to be granted, Archbishop Feehan, in 1901, appointed Father John Morris pastor of Saint Monica's. Mr. Peter Adler, Jr., the parish custodian, who was an usher in the church, and his mother lived in the small house formerly the home of Father Tolton and his mother.

From the time he took charge of Saint Monica's parish, Father Morris, with the help of lay women, gave catechetical instructions to the children after the Sunday Mass. The names of Mary A. Ryan, Mrs. Mary Alexander, and Mrs. Cora Spriggs are found in the records. The Sisters of Mercy, missioned at Saint Elizabeth's School, taught catechism classes in the black church to prepare children for First Communion.

The most far-reaching improvement that Father Morris made during his fifteen-year pastorate was the opening of Saint Monica's School. By this undertaking he not only met one of the most urgent needs of the parish, but he inaugurated a momentous movement in the cause of the education of black students.

Mother Katherine Drexel had continued to help the parish financially after Father Tolton's initial appeal and was now approached to take charge of Saint Monica's School. In 1912 Father Morris called on Mother Katherine at her convent in Cornwells Heights, Pennsylvania. Because he came at the request of James E. Quigley, then archbishop of Chicago, to ask for sisters, she immediately appointed five members of her community to take charge of Saint Monica's School. Father Morris rented an apartment for himself near the church and converted the rectory at 3669 South Wabash into a combined sisters' convent and parish school. A year later Mother Katherine purchased an old armory and remodeled it into a school because the convent was no longer adequate for the increased enrollment. Five years later Saint Monica's School merged with Saint Elizabeth's large grammar and high school and was staffed by additional Sisters of the Blessed Sacrament. Thus the appeals made to Mother Katherine, begun by Father Tolton, brought not only generous financial help but also the personal service of her sisters—a service still continued in three of Chicago's largest schools.

Father Morris soon realized that the black parishioners could not support the parish and school. Furthermore, the congregation was small—it had dwindled to fewer than one hundred persons since the death of Father Tolton four years earlier. To gain financial and moral support, Father Morris welcomed the white people of the neighborhood. "After his [Father Tolton's] death there was only a handful of Negro Catholics", writes Blanche Rodney, cited earlier. "The church was attended largely by whites. On Sundays it was so crowded, people had to stand. But after Cardinal Mundelein [then archbishop] came he had a chance to observe, and he took action. I remember reading a short article in the newspaper stating: 'In the future all whites are barred from Saint Monica's Church at 36th and Dearborn Streets.' It was quite a blow; they [the whites] were the main support of the parish.

I understand that a number of colored people reading the article thought it was prejudice; some were angered and left the church, but came back later; some never came back."

This racial antagonism, we recall, was already present in the time of Father Tolton and had become a matter of concern and suffering for him. The ill will tended to increase. Race consciousness was aroused more and more as blacks, unable to find room in Saint Monica's Church or because of distance and inconvenience, began to attend Mass regularly in the churches of their neighborhoods even in these places where they met with slight welcome and even open abuse. Then the whole situation was aggravated when blacks, coming from the South in ever greater numbers, looked for places of Catholic worship and opportunities for Catholic schooling.

George Cardinal Mundelein, who came to Chicago in 1916, was fully aware of the Church's obligation toward blacks, and he saw the need for action and the inauguration of a black apostolate. In 1917, he appointed the fathers of the Society of the Divine Word from Techny, Illinois, to take charge of Saint Monica's parish and to direct the work among Chicago's blacks. In the broadest sense of the word, Cardinal Mundelein gave the shepherdless flock "a pastor of their own".

The memory of Father Tolton is kept alive and has been revered by whites and blacks alike. On July 9, 1968, Brother Loyola Freightman, O.F.M., sacristan at Quincy College, wrote, "This morning I served the anniversary Mass that Father Landry Genosky celebrated for Father Augustine Tolton. It is seventy-one years ago that he died. . . .

"For me, the only colored Franciscan here, it was a great honor to assist at the Mass offered for the first Negro priest of the United States. May he rest in peace."

Father Tolton's death is listed, of course, in the official necrology of the diocese of Springfield in Illinois, containing a list of the deceased members of the clergy. It is also listed in the necrology of the archdiocese of Chicago's deceased clergy. Consequently he is remembered in the annual Mass celebrated by all the clergy of both dioceses.

There are other reminders that "the spirit of Father Tolton is marching on". Organizations dating from his day are living monuments to his leadership and influence. One of these is the Ladies Catholic Benevolent Association (L.C.B.A.), directed today [1973] by Mrs. Mamie Saunders. We learned earlier that Branch No. 67 of this association was encouraged by Father Tolton, directed by Mrs. Susie Wilson, and named Saint Monica's because Father Tolton was its first spiritual director.

Two years after the death of Father Tolton, the Women's Catholic Order of Foresters (W.C.O.F.) was established with Mrs. Cora Spriggs as leader. This fraternal society is still active today, and blazoned on its banner is: *Augustine Tolton Court No. 391.*

From 1897, the year of Father Tolton's death, to 1924, Saint Monica's Church served as a place of worship for parishioners, who continued to wonder when the building would be completed. "Mother Tolton", who continued as sacristan, died in 1911. Happily she was spared the painful experience of seeing the unfinished church abandoned in 1924 and finally (to make room for a city-planned housing project) demolished in 1945.

"That is where Saint Monica's Church used to be", says a present-day guide, pointing toward an immense housing project on Chicago's South Side. This maze of buildings has totally swallowed up 36th and Dearborn Streets and its environment; it has effaced all vestiges of Saint Monica's Church and rectory, and with it the grounds upon which were the earthly footprints of Father Tolton and his devoted mother.

The well-beaten path of Chicago's first black priest's world—a path beset with multiple problems of poverty, neglect, and racial difficulties—was paved over to provide a wider avenue for the multitudes of blacks coming from the South in search of money and jobs, homes to live in, and places to worship.

Even though all traces of his sojourn in Chicago's South Side have been obliterated, Father Tolton's name has been perpetuated and with it the principles which motivated his Christian life. The last pastor of Saint Monica's Church, Father Joseph Eckert, S.V.D., was blessed in generous measure with an intuitive love and understanding of the blacks. His parishioners quickly sensed that his interest in them was of the kind that took no note of color or race; that it was something purely Christian—something that he could neither feign nor conceal. His black congregations in Chicago outgrew each one of the large parish churches to which he had been assigned: Saint Monica's, Saint Elizabeth's, and Saint Anselm's. Because of his firmness, sense of justice, and compassion, the blacks saw in him Father Tolton's true image, and they bestowed on him the highest accolade that their experience dictated: the second Father Tolton. Thus the compliment paid to the last pastor of Saint Monica's Church served to perpetuate the name of the first pastor.

The need for the sterling qualities of the "second Father Tolton" continued to increase. Saint Monica's Church, which had been planned for expansion, was destined never to be completed. However, even though the building had been finished in the elaborate design that Father Tolton and his helpers had planned, the space would still have been inadequate for the increasing number of Chicago's black Catholics. This increase in black population after the turn of the century demanded not only a larger church but also more and more churches.

The coming of blacks from the South just before and during World War I was indeed quite spectacular. In the years 1917 and 1918 alone a thousand new arrivals per day jammed into Chicago's black district. By 1935 there were 240,000 blacks in the city. This continuing influx brought problems of living space; it forced the blacks out of their ghettos into the areas formerly occupied by the whites. Real estate dealers called the movement an "invasion". The word frightened many white people, causing them to leave their homes and settle in other parts of the city or in the suburbs.

The flight of the whites, an interesting chapter in Chicago's history of Catholicism, meant that magnificent churches and well-equipped schools were left to the black Catholics. But more than that! It is to the enduring credit of the priests that they did not join the flight of the whites. They remained steadfast in their posts to minister to the new contingent of the people of God.

In the tradition of Father Tolton, these priests encouraged blacks and whites to worship God as one people. Consequently, color and race had no place in their plans and ministry, just as they had no place in the apostolate of the first Negro priest, who, as we recall, "after six years in Rome . . . had not completely realized the difference between white and black".

During the whole period of adjustment, pastors and assistants were reassured and supported by Cardinal Samuel Stritch, who, in 1939, made the significant proclamation: "Every church, school, and institution of this archdiocese is open to Catholic people, Negroes, whites, and all other nationalities."

From the time he came to Chicago until his death in 1958, Cardinal Stritch encouraged and befriended black people. His sincere high regard for them is found in the address which he gave before a black audience in New Orleans:

> The only native artistic culture that we may boast of in the United States is the culture that you have given us in your music and folklore, and that culture is filled with the thoughts and atmosphere of God. . . . You have brought honor to the Catholic name in the United States, and you have given us a hope and a promise from which there will come great and powerful things in the future.

This "hope and promise" were to be fulfilled: The work of the "Second Father Tolton" did not end with his nineteen-year apostolate in Chicago. Father Joseph Eckert became rector of Saint Augustine Seminary, Bay Saint Louis, Mississippi—the center which has trained and ordained more than two hundred black priests within three decades. Furthermore, this number included Harold R. Perry, auxiliary bishop of New Orleans, Louisiana, who was consecrated in 1965.

In a talk at the Divine Word Seminary, Epworth, Iowa, in January 1967, Bishop Perry said that he was pastor of an integrated parish in New Orleans which is three-fourths white. He added that his parishioners are proud to have a bishop as their pastor and that they are not concerned about the color of his skin.

These are the "great and wonderful things" that Cardinal Stritch predicted would come about. These are the results of the efforts made by pioneers such as Father Tolton and all those who worked with him and after him. Many of these leaders have followed the spirit of the first black priest of the United States: a spirit that moved the people of God to work side by side. They realize Father Augustine Tolton's ideal when they put into practice the words he so often spoke: "We do not tell people to go out of the church; we tell them to go in."

BIBLIOGRAPHY

Bruener, Theodore. *Kirchengeschichte Quincy's*. St. Louis: B. Herder and Company, 1887.

Buehrle, Maria C. *The Cardinal Stritch Story*. Milwaukee: Bruce Publishing Company, 1959.

Burton, Katherine. *The Golden Door*. New York: P. J. Kenedy and Sons, 1957.

Drake, St. Clair. *Churches and Voluntary Associations*. Chicago: University of Chicago Press, 1940.

Foley, Albert S., S.J. *God's Men of Color*. New York: Farrar, Strauss and Company, 1955.

Frazier, Franklin E. *The Negro Family in Chicago*. Chicago: University of Chicago Press, 1923.

Gillard, Rev. John T., S.S.J. *The Catholic Church and the Negro*. Baltimore: St. Joseph's Society Press, 1929.

Goebel, Bernardin, O.F.M. *Seven Steps to the Altar*. New York: Sheed and Ward, 1963.

Habig, Marion A., O.F.M. *Heralds of the King*. Chicago: Franciscan Herald Press, 1958.

Hayes, Hazel. *The Growth of the Negro Institutions in Chicago*. Chicago: University of Chicago Press, 1940.

Heston, Edward L., C.S.C. *The Holy See at Work*. Milwaukee: Bruce Publishing Company, 1950.

Mundelein, Most Rev. George William, D.D. *Two Crowded Years*. Extension Press, 1918.

Reuter, Edward B. *The Mulatto in the United States*. New York: Thomas Y. Crowell and Company, 1918.

Stampp, Kenneth M. *The Peculiar Institution*. New York: Random House, 1956.

Thompson, Joseph J., comp. and ed. *Diocese of Springfield in Illinois: Diamond Jubilee History*. Springfield, Ill.: Rt. Rev. James A. Griffin, D.D. (Springfield, Ill.: Hartman Printing, 1928).

Zimmerman, Rev. Aloysius, S.V.D. *The Beginning of an Era*. Chicago: Illinois Press, 1952.

Articles

Duren, Stephen. "The First American Colored Priest". *Interracial Review*, May 1935.

Eckert, Joseph F., S.V.D. "The Negro in Chicago". *Our Colored Missions*, January 1937.

Genosky, Rev. Landry, O.F.M. "Father Augustine Tolton". *Vandalia Intelligencer*, 1966.

Greene, Rev. John H., S.S.J. "The Reverend Augustine Tolton". *St. Joseph's Advocate*, October and July 1866, January and April 1887, January and April 1888.

Hemesath, Sister Mary Caroline, O.S.F. "The Crossing". *Ave Maria*, May 21, 1966.

———."Mission Work among the Negroes in Chicago". *Our Colored Missions*, August 25, 1925.

———."White Policy toward the Chicago Negro, 1865–1941" (unpublished master's dissertation, Catholic University, Washington, D.C., 1941).

Howard, Mrs. Oliver. "Augustine Tolton". *Quincy Herald Whig*, September 30, 1962.

Quincy College Bulletin. "Stroll through Old Graveyard Stirs Memories". *Falcon*, Quincy, Illinois, October 13, 1931.

Reily, John T. "A Page from History". *Our Colored Missions*, June 1945.

Souvenir of the Diamond Jubilee of St. Boniface Congregation, Quincy, Illinois, 1837–1912.

Steins, Richard H. "The Mission of the Josephites to the Negro in America, 1871–1893" (unpublished master's dissertation, Columbia University, New York, 1966).

Wiegland, Joseph C. "Brush Creek Gave U.S. First Negro Priest". *Catholic Missourian*, April 27, 1958.

Wolf, F. "Franciscan Negro Parish". *The Gleaner*, Westmont, Illinois, April, 1937.

Wood, Junius B. "The Negro in Chicago". *The Chicago Daily News*, December 11, 1916.

Letters to the Author

Alphonse, Mother M., O.S.B.S., St. Elizabeth's Convent, Cornwells Heights, Penn., March 16, 1966.

Antonice, Mother Mary, S.S.N.D., Notre Dame on the Lake, Mequon, Wisconsin.

Biocchi, D. A., Assistant Archivist, Sacred Congregation of the Propagation of the Faith, Rome, Italy, May 3, 1966, with the following enclosures:

Prefect of the Sacred Congregation to the Reverend Janssen, administrator of the diocese of Alton, June 16, 1886.

Sacred Congregation to Father Augustine Tolton: September 8, 1886; August 29, 1887; November 7, 1889.

Father Augustine Tolton to the prefect of the Sacred Congregation: September 1, 1886; July 25, 1887; July 12, 1889; September 4, 1889; October 7, 1889.

Prefect of the Sacred Congregation to Bishop Ryan; November 7, 1889.—Bishop Ryan to the Sacred Congregation: November 18, 1889.

Covelli, R. F., Secretary of Archdiocese of Chicago Chancery, February 1, 1966.

Davis, Mrs. Bertina (pioneer member of St. Elizabeth's parish, Chicago, Illinois), August 14, 1966.

Eckert, Rev. Joseph, S.V.D., Rector of Saint Augustine Seminary, Bay St. Louis, Mississippi, August 30, 1941.

Felicitas, Sister Mary, S.F.P., Superior-Administrator of Saint Mary's Hospital, Hoboken, New Jersey, July 18, 1966, and July 30, 1966.

Hogan, Rev. Peter E., S.S.J., Archivist, Baltimore, Maryland, December 23, 1965, and August 4, 1966.

Hubbard-Barnett, Mrs. Caecilia (member of Father Tolton's parish), Long Island City, New York, October 4, 1966, and December 16, 1966.

Pallikaparampil, Rev. Joseph, Assistant Rector of the *Collegio Urbano de Propaganda Fide*, Rome, Italy, March 21, 1966.

Raymonda, Sister Mary, R.S.M., R.R.L., Medical Records Librarian, Mercy Hospital, Chicago, Illinois, September 28, 1966.

Rodney, Mrs. Blanche (member of Saint Monica's parish), Chicago, Illinois, October 2, 1966.

Newspapers

The Catholic Missourian, April 27, 1958.

The Chicago Daily News, July 9, 1897; July 10, 1897; July 12, 1897; July 13, 1897.

The Chicago Defender, October 7, 1939; April 13, 1945.

The Chicago Tribune, July 12, 1897.

The New World, April 16, 1937; October 3, 1936; August 16, 1938; July 17, 1939; July 12, 1940.

Quincy *Herald-Whig*, September 30, 1962.

The Quincy *Journal*, June 13, 1880; July 19, 1886; July 25, 1886; July 26, 1886; July 10, 1897; July 12, 1897; August 9, 1897.

INDEX